for the sick and tired
who are sick and tired
of being sick and tired

WHO'S THE MATTER WITH ME?

By Alice Steadman

An oyster takes an
irritation and makes
of it a pearl. How
many pearls could
we make in a week?

Alice Steadman

DeVorss & Company
P.O. BOX 550, MARINA DEL REY, CA 90294-0550

First Edition 1966
Eighth Revised Edition 1977
Thirteenth Printing 1986

May be quoted in part if source and supply address are given.

ISBN: 0-87516-225-8

Published by
DeVorss & Company
P.O. Box 550
Marina del Rey, California   90294-0550

Printed in the United States of America

This book is dedicated to my Mother,
Alice Slate Tuttle,

*who, during her full life in a small doctorless town, adminis-
tered with love her simple home remedies while she listened to
her friends' "druthers" and "bothers"; to my friends who
shared their views on their pains and problems; and to Sylvia
McInvaill, who taught me how to know myself.*

*And my additions to the second edition to Paul, a misfit
who wrote at the beginning of the Piscean Age the wisdom that
will be better understood in the beginning of this Aquarian
Age and who said, "When I came to you, my brothers, to
preach God's secret truths to you I did not use long words and
great learning." – I Cor. 2:1.*

*"God purposely chose what the world considers nonsense
in order to put wise men to shame, and what the world considers weak in order to put powerful men to shame. He chose
what the world looks down on, and despises, and thinks is
nothing, in order to destroy what the world thinks is important." – I Cor 1:27-29.*

(From Good News for Modern Man version.)

CONTENTS

INTRODUCTION

Suppose one glaring light is shining in your eyes, blinding you on your "stage." You are told that here are ten thousand switches, one of which will cut it off and if you will say which one, it shall be cut off. Our body responses are as mysterious to the average person as that light panel is to a two-year-old. This book attempts to reveal to you many of those switches, so that you may cut off an unwanted annoyance as soon as it appears.

We should not have to call in an electrician each time a switch should be cut off or a fuse should be changed, but it is also foolish for an amateur to do important electrical work and endanger the house. So, on your way to the doctor, give some thought to the emotion that may have triggered the pain or the disease.

Pain can be created in the body when that which your soul thinks is the right thing to do still gets no cooperation from the body, or when the body, or human desire, insists on doing things that make the soul sick.

This book assumes that you believe you have a soul and, since everything made has a purpose, the soul has a purpose. "Our birth is but a sleep and a forgetting" of what that purpose is. Your body is constantly revealing your purpose to you, if you will but listen and understand its whisperings. The inner man is in constant "conversation" with the outer man.

i

We seem not to be able to believe this unless we have pains. Some of us need a sound jolt from that "inner self." The body becomes a battleground of arguments and a site of peace treaties. "Let not the sun go down on your wrath." If the day ends with the peace treaty instead of a truce, there is general good health, but there are ways to eliminate these constant "wars and rumors of wars." You point the finger at "who" is the matter with you — but at whom are the other fingers pointing?

It has been proved by medical clinics that approximately seventy per cent of the patients who come to them have emotionally-induced ailments. This book is aimed at the relief and solution of a few ailing patients who would really wish to be the master of their own body and whose doctor has said there is no organic reason for the pain.

Through my interest in preventive medicine I have been a listener to thousands of accounts of aches and pains, with their accompanying personality conflicts. In one of his books U. S. Anderson said that there must be a key to why one person under stress will have a stomach ache and another will have his heart act up. So, I began the search for the "Who" that causes the "What" on that intricate machine, the body.

Loring T. Swaim, M.D., in his book *Arthritis and the Spiritual Laws,* found that when he used the approved methods to relieve his rheumatic and arthritic patients, improvement was slow and recurrences were too frequent. Finally he found that when the patient would apply the spiritual laws of love and forgiveness, the active disease subsided and remained so for unusually long periods. Recurrence seemed to come when a new or old emotional hurt was indulged.

Most of the ideas of this book are well known to psychiatrists and medical doctors. If the excellent books written on the correlation of mind and body were read by those who seek a clue to their pains, there would be less reason to have compiled these body-soul relationships. But most of the books are voluminous and the clues are sometimes veiled in medical terms which the layman does not understand.

The "ulcer-patient" type has in his *total* case history all the bothers he has ever had in his personality and environment. Many of these would have been resolved in his mind in a normal way and would not be the cause of a body ailment. A few of these unresolved conflicts could trigger the ulcer, and if the patient knew which ones were the cause he would be glad to change his mind. The quicker you can "catch" and reverse a negative thought, the sooner your body will become well.

*

"Take my life and let it be
   Consecrated, Lord, to Thee;
Take my moments and my days —
   Let them flow in ceaseless praise.
Take my hands and let them move
   At the impulse of Thy love;
Take my feet and let them be
   Swift and beautiful for Thee.
Take my voice and let me sing,
   Always only for my King.
Take my intellect and use
   Every power as Thou shall choose.
Take my will and make it Thine;
   It shall be no longer mine.
Take myself and I will be
   Ever, only, all for Thee."

F. R. Havergal — 1847

The Golden Age, 1000 years of Peace, can come when every person knows himself as God's child and every other person his brother, and a teacher of a lesson he needs to learn.

WHO'S THE MATTER WITH ME?

People of different temperaments are predisposed to different ailments, because their "druthers" and their "bothers" are different. The places on and in your body that are consistently sensitive are trying to tell you that you are going against your soul purposes. As your mother tapped your hand that was reaching into the forbidden cookie jar, so our soul spanks us with pain in the part of the body that is the symbol of the wrong thought or act. It's as simple as understanding why you get your finger bitten when you stick it in another's face.

You will learn to read these messages. You will be able to answer these age-old questions: Why was I born? What is my soul's purpose? Why do I have this particular ailment? Why did this happen to me?

It is amazing to see how people use parts of the body to express opinions about self or others. This can give you a clue to "what" as well as "who" frustrates you. For instance, listen to this negative organ recital:

"He gives me a headache."

"I couldn't face it." "I lost face in my group."

"She looks down her nose at me." "I turn up my nose at that."

"We do not see *eye* to *eye*." "I (eye) can't see that."

1

"I can't swallow that."

"I've bitten off more than I can swallow."

"He'd cut my throat."

"He's a pain in the neck."

"It makes my heart ache."

"Get it off your chest." "Don't breathe a word of it."

"He has no backbone." "It's breaking my back."

"I will not bend my knee to them."

"I resist being changed." (stiffness)

"Don't step on my feet." (Having another underfoot hurts.)

"They are elbowing me out of my place."

"They are putting the finger on me."

If you didn't say it, did you think it? Unexpressed thoughts can lie buried in your emotional "brain" and like the needle on a broken record wear the groove in you deep, deep, deep. The body has no sense of humor and hears only words of action.

We do not think with just our conscious brain, although the brain *is* the switchboard through which impulses go. We think with *every* cell and gland in our body. Mind is in every one of the trillion cells; as the brain is the switchboard of the conscious mind, so the solar plexus is the "brain" of feeling and sensation, or of the subconscious mind. The solar plexus — possibly not commonly known — is a group of twelve nerves situated just back of the stomach and the nerves fan out to all parts of the body. Hurt feelings can feel as if it were the stomach.

Thought and Body

Every thought we have has an instant effect on some part of our body. If the thought calls for action, we can see it. We also see blushing and turning pale, but the thoughts we do not express outwardly are buried within the body cells, and if they are unpleasant they show only in our ailments, our aches, our pains, our grunts, and our groans. One person sees red artificial roses and is reminded of one of his happiest moments. Another, seeing the same roses, recalls the most despondent day of his life and starts sneezing.

Our cells, including glands, have recorded in them all our past thoughts and emotions and experiences. Our daily thoughts play upon that recording and if we do not learn to erase the unpleasant memories, the "tune" our body "plays" is out of harmony.*

Emerson says, "If you would see a person's soul, look at his body." The body is a visible picture of what you think of your world. Suffering shows that you are out of harmony with some part of it.

Alexis Carrel says in *Man the Unknown,* "So completely and wonderfully made is the human body that there is nothing in the outer world that does not have a miniature replica within it." Your body is your universe.

Think of this wonderful vehicle, your body, and know that you are the only one that can have full mastery over it. In an emergency the doctors, the psychiatrists, your pastor, loved ones, drugs, herbs, and medicines can help balance the body. But only you can keep it balanced.

When I say you, I mean the total you — Body, Mind, and Soul working in harmony with the Spirit within. The unification of purpose of all these is the new birth; it seems as though you are a new creature.

It is important that you know that you are more than your body. You are Spirit made Man-i-fest, the dwelling place of the

---

* "Emotions indulged in for a prolonged time actually create tissue changes in the organ or organ system involved." Dr. H. F. Dunbar in *Emotions and Bodily Changes.* New York: Columbia University Press.

Spirit of God, the vehicle through which the soul can fulfill its purpose, and you are mind made free and creative by the love of the Creator, with the potential of all the creative power of the Son of God, which you are. This is what Christ told us. You are a soul which came into the world for a very special purpose. These are the things you really are. Eliminate either one and your eye (I) is not single and your body not radiant with spirit-filled light. Like a TV with three tuning devices, they must be synchronized to get the right picture.

You, all of you, are a very special part of a great Universal Plan, and you are a soul living on *this* earth and in *this* body to perform a task that only you can do. If one took a cup of water from the ocean, all the waters of the world would have to move over to fill the gap. You *are* important; the world would not be the same without you.

Job lamented that man who is born of woman is of few days. This is the human body. But man is also born of God, and that part is eternal. There is no death; there is only life visible and invisible.

There are two creations of man as recorded in Genesis. The first is the creative divine man made with the imagination and creativeness of his Maker. However, man desired a closer relationship with his world, and "God took clay" (the minerals and elements of the earth) and made man a body. Man's body can be reduced back to the elements of the earth, but the spirit and soul that is of the nature of God is eternal.

Mind acts as a coordinator between body and spirit.

The tremendous power which we have isn't easy to manage at times without coming close to disaster or great sickness, unless it remains in constant alignment with its Maker through the Spirit within.

Many writers have described Life as a journey. So imagine, if you will, the driver (the conscious mind) in charge of trillions of horses (cells). This is greater than the twenty-mule team you see on television. The driver tries to keep them under control. The Spirit is within the carriage, willing and waiting to be called upon for instant control; but since Man has free will, Spirit does not intrude because we must ask for it. The soul, in the carriage, knowing its purpose for life's journey, is also connected with every cell through glandular action and the sympathetic nervous system. This conscious mind of ours fails to heed the voice of the soul or seek advice from the Spirit. The soul is sick to see its life's journey wasted in meanderings that lead it no closer to perfection.

When wrong thinking misdirects the cells, right thinking brings them back into harmony. In some people this has been instantaneous; in others it's a slow process, because they are so stubborn. In the Spirit there is no time or space; there is only *now.*

When unruly cells are not commanded rightly by you, they can be "unhitched," or cut out by a surgeon. Many cells of our body are expendable, because other cells will take their place; but if the thought is not changed and wrong commands are given to them, then the new cells also become unruly. There was a time the heart could not be discarded, but medical doctors with God's spirit have overcome that, and man if left a small piece of liver can grow another. The spirit of good is already within every cell awaiting your faith and your command. "Before you call, I have answered." "As you believe, so it is done unto you." "Thy faith has made you whole." "God specializes in things thought impossible." Prayer about anything is like holding a magnifying glass over it. It concentrates what was already there to the point in question.

Disease Is Friction

Disease is caused by friction or stress between two of our selves, between the body and the soul. The soul knows the purpose for which it came and, when it realizes that the human part of us is not cooperating, it becomes sick. We could cry,

"My soul is sick," and say with Paul, "The things I should do I don't do, and the things I shouldn't I do."

We were made to be co-creators with the Father and we each create *after our own kind.* Our mistake is made by putting unlike elements together. The results are called by many names; war, divorce, disease, unhappiness, and explosions. What God (Good) has put together *no man can put asunder.* We put things together without using God's wisdom and then cry, "Man must not put asunder!" For the sake of our happiness, we must realize that we can never lose anything that belongs to us, nor can we possess what is not really ours. We are prone to think we possess people, or things, because we legally own them, but real love is the only thing that can bind anything to us. If we have that, the other so-called problems are nothing.

Where Is Man's Divinity?

A story is told in mythology of how the gods tried to decide where to hide man's divinity, that he might not find it until he searched for it with his whole heart. Some said to hide it in outer space, or deep within the earth, or in deep waters; but the wisest one said that the human side of man would conquer space, waters, and earth, and that the best place to hide man's divinity is within himself, for that is the last place man would think to look for it. When the world needed help in knowing this, the Perfect Son told them, "Go within". . ."Be still and know". . . "The kingdom of heaven is within". . .but only a few understood when He said we are all sons of God, co-creators with the Father, and that what He did we could do; and many insist we are "worms" and that it would be presumptuous to believe that God loves us *no matter how bad we are.* Christ came to show us the way, that although human, we also were the dwelling place of the Father. He showed us that God did not condemn us; we condemned ourselves. He healed by seeing the perfection within those who came to Him with faith.

Remember that even Jesus was not able to do any good works in the towns where people did not believe He could. Yet you hear one curse God for his miseries and say, "If He knew what I should have had, why didn't He give it to me?" The air that gives you life is there for the using, but even God can't make you breathe if you decide not to. God works through us according to the purposes of our soul.

"It is done unto you as you believe it will be done unto you." What you really believe in your soul. It's as simple as that, and therein lies the key to all our joys and all our sorrows. Whatever we think about consistently with emotion we will attract to us. Or we could say we attract what we are, our loves and our fears. We have to be strong to keep the negative bombardments of our thoughts and of the world from affecting us. We alone are the creators of our inner world, and the outer world is but a reflection of it. When television commercials say, "Do you have tired blood?" yell "No! My blood is renewed at the rate of twenty million cells per second and lives only twenty-one days and isn't old enough to be tired." Whenever the over-forty routine makes you sag, remember that medical science has found that it takes only eleven months or less for a cell to be remade from start to finish and that in the matter of a year or so no part of your body is the same as it was. If you look like you did eleven months ago or a few years ago, it is because you are thinking pretty much as you did then. Have you not seen a person so changed by great joy or deep sorrow that in a year's time you hardly knew him? Do not re-do your termite weakened structure with weak, worm-eaten timbers.

If one could think *only* beautiful, God-like thoughts for a whole year, one would *be* beautiful no matter what the original looked like.

If we are to have any control over our body, we must stop reacting blindly to stimuli; we must become aware of the association between emotions and bodily reactions. It will explain why you can get a cold when you are not thinking of a cold. It will even explain why you get a flat tire or other car trouble when you were not thinking of car troubles. This you will understand later. It is known as a reflex action or a "scapegoat."

Criticism Boomerangs

This knowledge of cause and effect, like all great laws of nature, is a two-edged knife that can cut the one mis-using it. If you use it other than to understand the problems of yourself and your fellow man and the animal world, so that through love you can help them back onto the Path to Perfection, then you will "turn" it on yourself. As a result, you will tend to take on the ailments symbolical of those you criticize or refuse to understand, or are over-sympathetic with. We must do what we can — love the person and let the Spirit of God have its way with the situation.

Soul Builds Its Own House

Emerson said, "Each soul builds itself a body." In the nine months before birth and during the years of infancy, the emotional mind of the baby is impressed by the parents and whoever else is caring for it. Many sickly children "grow out of it" when they start using their own minds instead of being torn emotionally between conflicting minds. Those that survive are stronger physically as an adult than the "hot-house" variety, because they have learned to overcome the world (race mind), the flesh (body), and those devilish brands of wrong thinking.

No matter what kind of body is created by the parents, it is chosen by the soul under divine direction as its earthly vehicle near the time of birth. So says Edgar Cayce, one of the world's greatest mystics. It is a bit like a person needing a type of transportation and choosing one according to his purposes. Each person's needs are different and where one may choose a mule for narrow paths and rough terrain, another person may need a Cadillac or a rowboat or a battleship, or even a jet plane.

What is right for one may be a handicap to another. Many a wonderful soul chooses a so-called handicapped body because, through it, its purposes can best be accomplished. A Phillips screwdriver is useless if you need the usual type, or an extension ladder is a handicap when you need a five-foot ladder. Many a budding mechanic prefers to acquire a dilapidated car and rebuild it to suit his purpose.

As a balloon is compressed at one place to increase the inflation at another, so it seems many souls have chosen to take compressed or deformed bodies for special purposes. Socrates was bow-legged and pigeon-chested, Milton was blind, Aesop a slave and a hunchback, Helen Keller — blind, deaf, and dumb — is one of the most wonderful personalities in the world. An Armenian boy, spastic born, with no use of hands or legs, is one of the world's most brilliant scientists.

Soul Has a Purpose

Sometimes a soul accomplishes its purpose in a very short time, as we reckon time. I know that the soul that came to Dale and Roy Rogers fulfilled its mission beautifully and wonderfully, and its mission could probably only have been done in a so-called handicapped body. This girl child was an angel of love and enlightenment to literally thousands of people although she lived only a few short years on this planet. Love of children was so increased in her parents that they adopted many "unadoptable" children.

I like to think that the two children who drowned in a mudhole in Charlotte, North Carolina, also fulfilled their purposes. They were small, unloved and neglected, and their presence was not missed; but because of the manner of their passing, the City of Charlotte realized that their life-saving equipment was extremely inadequate. More equipment and a new ambulance were bought. These children gave their lives that others might live, just as nobly as any soldier on a battlefield.

Edgar Cayce says that not only would a soul choose a body it feels will best equip him for his purpose, but it chooses the race, family and environment that would be best to work out these purposes. You *asked* to be born; you chose your vehicle and potential experiences under divine guidance. What progress have you made since you came?

To have a purpose does not mean that every person *is* working on his purpose. Wordsworth says, "Our birth is but a sleep and a forgetting." Many a student starts to a school with his purpose well defined, but distractions occupy his time until he may find he has wasted many years.

Have you never gone into a grocery store for one special item, like paprika? You do not make a list because anybody can remember *one* item. You meet with several friends, and you put many other items in your basket because you will need them in a few days. When you get home, you do not have the thing you most wanted for a special purpose.

If you come to a mature realization of your soul's real purpose, then don't waste time by berating yourself for wasted years. Instead of thinking of them as wasted, think of them as training for your soul's purpose. I know a man who spent his first forty years as a bum, a wanderer, a collector of knowledge from every type of undesirable companion, a drunkard. When his soul got the "upper hand," he became a great spiritual leader for alcoholics. He used his knowledge of every conceivable emotion to be able to understand his "patients."

If you have come to an awareness that you are no longer satisfied with you as you are, your soul is "talking" to you. Listen to it. In every imperfect person there is a perfect person trying to express himself. The "mistakes" you have made were necessary for your own perfection. The wisest people are those who have made the most mistakes and learned from them.

Sit down and make a list of your real aim or aims in life. You may find that you are not working towards them at all, or not consistently.

If a soul chooses a body to help work out its purpose and then proceeds to build and rebuilt it for its own purpose, it can explain why so many adopted children are like their adopted parents. I like to think that when there is a physical reason why a soul cannot be born to its true soul parents, it takes a rundabout way to get to them. It goes to a mother it knows will release it to its "true" mother. We have all been amazed that an adopted child has as many physical and mental characteristics as a natural child might possess.

Sometimes identical twins have souls with similar purposes and the circumstances of their lives appear the same, but it's possible that the two souls occupying identical twins' bodies are not of the same purpose and their bodies could become less alike as time goes on.

There are times when two people who are very compatible do not look alike. They are like the paper heart cut apart for a Valentine party and you find your partner by finding the other part of your heart. Some people are of such complex make-up that they can only be compatible with those who have what they lack. By working together they are a complete whole. When they try to make over the other to be like themselves, they defeat themselves.

As "soul mates" are attracted to each other because of their sameness or differences, so other people come into our lives as we need them for the furthering of our knowledge and experiences. *Any person that comes into our life has done so to teach us or learn from us.* If it seems to be an unpleasant association, learn the lesson within it quickly and it will "go away." "Whatever you bless blesses you; whatever you curse curses you."

Problems Must Be Confronted

Never run from a problem; either it will chase you or, like a cop who calls ahead of the speeder, you run into another just like it, although it has a different face and name.

Many a man or woman has divorced a mate because of certain quirks of personality, and married another with the same qualities, which he discovers later. If you desire to change your spouse, change yourself, and he will change. That's the only way. But don't "sell your soul" to change him or her.

Many a girl has eloped to get away from a domineering parent and found herself married to a domineering husband.

It has been said, and I repeat, that we can change only ourselves and if we do, then our world, our circumstances, seem to be changed. If you do not like your world, change yourself to what you would wish and you will attract those things and people you wish. Like attracts like. You cannot change your image in the mirror by smashing the mirror.

James Allen in *As a Man Thinketh* says, "Circumstance does not make the man, it reveals him to himself." Blame no one but yourself for the conditions surrounding you. There is a purpose in it. Work your way out of it and in so doing you become a greater person. This Earth planet is but a proving ground for higher dimensions. It has been said that the cause of all disease is the soul's frustrated desire for a special perfection. Your idea of perfection is different from that of another; thus, your frustration being different, your disease is different. A person doing what he knows he must, and allowing no one's opinion to short-circuit that flow, is not bothered by the aches and pains that "dog" those who bury their hurts and fears within, as a dog buries its bones.

How to overcome it? Shall you hurt another, voice opinions you would rather die (and do die) than say? Not necessarily; anything you can think you can "unthink." "Transform your body by the renewing of your mind," said Paul. Others' opinions and criticisms may have in them a germ of truth you need; if not, forget it. Since you become what you consistently think about, make a list of your thoughts and you will see your becoming portrait. If you could stop thinking of what you do not like and think of the perfection desired, your body would become more perfect. If you are capable of an emotion that makes you sick, you *can* have the opposite emotion that makes you well.

Most people do not desire a drastic change; they want their friends to still recognize them. They would like to change from tiredness to vitality, from occasional head- and backaches and colds to optimum health. You can, if you will, change the emotion that caused that particular pain. Take your mind off the mistakes and know you are forgiven; then center your mind on the ideal your soul knows. God forgives you as you forgive yourself.

When you have changed the thought that triggered the emotion that caused the aches, then keep it changed. When you throw out the garbage, don't go fingering into it for bits around which to build your next meal. We do just that when we "dig up" those old hurts and fears and wallow in the miseries of the past. "Let the *dead past* bury its dead" while you go on to new glories.

Thoughts Have Wings

We should realize that every thought goes out as an electric vibration and is received by those in tune and then comes back to us magnified. Burbank said it should be as illegal to think a hateful thought and pollute the air people must breathe as to poison water people must drink.

Make a mental picture of a thought or word projected into the ethers above you. Picture it as a lovely cloud of light when it is a good thought, or smog if it is discordant. Now see the earth spinning through this beautiful or polluted ether until, in one revolution of twenty-four hours, it has touched every person in every land. When we realize that the unrest of every community, city, and nation is vibrating in the ethers and everyone "picks up" the vibrations to which he is attuned, we realize why the world is so jittery.

"What can I do?" you ask. There is only one Power, one God, and beside Him there is no other. "Thou shalt have no other gods before Me." Any power other than God has only the amount of power *you* give it; so take away that power by sending out constructive thoughts of love and understanding and know that in every creature there is the spirit of God that can be released and is receptive to your good thoughts. Mentally release that power for good, and know that the world is a better place because of your thought. "One person on the side of God is a majority." As a great poet said, "Let everyone sweep his own doorstep and every doorstep will be clean." Start peace where you are, within your family, your neighborhood, and so on out into the world.

A Balanced Life Is Difficult

The good that we are and that we would do is like the lovely flower that springs from a bulb which has within it all the beauty and purpose it will ever need. In order to be a part of this world, however, the bulb must flourish in this world and be physically nourished by the physical world of soil and water, sunshine and air. As it pushes up into the air it comes in contact with all the things that have been planted for ages past, both useful and useless for us, good and bad for us; we could call this the race mind, or opinions which consist of cans and can'ts. We must weed out and keep on weeding out these wrong ideas. Probably the hardest decision is which is the better of two good decisions. Two equally lovely flowers side by side may choke each other. The morning glories in the rose bed, for instance. Ask for divine guidance and know that you have it; then do what you think you must do. You'll make mistakes, but you will learn from them.

"In this world we will have tribulations"; but do not despair. It can be overcome by love which manifests as right living and, of course, right thinking. Christ did it and said His way was easy and that His way caused the burden to be no burden at all. Our problems are our crosses, our victories the crowns.

Just as you cannot harvest apples from pear trees, so you cannot think evil thoughts and reap good deeds. It will show either in your worldly affairs or in your body. You have seen circumstances which may at the surface seem otherwise, but a person is not all bad and it is very difficult to be all good. It is possible for a farmer to grow wonderful corn and for some reason he doesn't do well with potatoes. A man may live a saintly life, yet harbor a long-standing resentment or perhaps guilt for some childhood thought which he will not forget, and it literally eats his vitals out. Every man has many possible facets in his "diamonds", and many are not polished. A man can be an ideal boss and businessman, but as a father he seems a failure; a friend to all strangers, but a stranger in his own home. A man can love a daughter and hate a son; or he can give love to the downtrodden races and fail as a husband.

This business of total balance is a difficult state to achieve.

In times long ago a couple would raise sheep for clothing and food. They spun the thread, wove the cloth and made the clothes; and the pride in all their achievements and their feeling of being needed was a bulwark against the emotional conflicts which this generation builds up.

Now you can make a telephone call or push a button and all your bodily needs are cared for, and your soul feels cheated unless you find the non-material reasons for being needed. I cannot feel that the progress we have made in the mechanical age, which eliminates the tasks of yesteryears, has as its purpose to fill institutions to overflowing with people who now feel useless, unneeded, and unloved. Without purpose they have forgotten *who* they are as the son of the Creator and that the Way is the Path of unconditional love.

We were released from menial drudgery because we had the potential of greater work, of higher consciousness, and we must find it if we want wholeness.

We no longer live in the world where we must do everything to be complete (whole). We now live in a world of brotherhood, and we live for and by and with each other. One God, one world, God in every one of His children and in everything. "There is no spot where God is not."

Let us look at life's many facets or expressions this way: We live in a world where there are four basic elements: air, fire, earth, and water. And if we are not happily balanced, it may be for need of one or more of these qualities. For those who are too "fiery" or nervous there is water therapy, or earth will slow up the fire, or we could sometimes give it air, air it out, and let it burn itself out. Being near slow or rhythmical water helps smooth out the system for too-busy and nervous people. As they watch the breakers come one after the other, they begin to realize there's no need to exhaust themselves on each one; there will be another and another. Opportunities will always come if you are ready for them, and peace within will attract more than frantic rushing and grabbing. Know that water has the power to hold you up if you quietly let it. Let go and let good come to you. Sitting quietly near a litter of puppies, your own will come to you, but if you dash around noisily none will.

Then there are those who have overdone the nature of water, which seeks the horizontal position. Then in order to get the best of their nature, we must warm or heat it to produce steam to get action. Those people who are bored, phlegmatic and aimless may be told to get more rest, which is what they don't need; they need to be stirred, to be even made angry until they use the potentials of their nature. Like Mr. Borden, who was so angry when babies died on an ocean voyage because the cows became sick that he found a way to can milk for all future babies.

Then there are those who are too airy and must be brought down to earth; their "outer space" ideas must be given a practical use. Other too-airy types air their views too quickly to too many and need to compress some of it to get power, just as a stream must be dammed for a reservoir of power.

Air must be "fired" at times to raise it for certain purposes, or cooled to get other qualities.

To air out a place or ideas, purifies, provided the air replacing it is pure.

The fourth element is earth, and to be down-to-earth and practical is good — provided you don't get in the ruts which are not taking you where you want to go. Earth is your home, but the heavenly state should be your destination.

Earth without water is unproductive, whereas too much water with earth results in mud. Earth without the warmth of the sun is a breeding place of undesirable molds, whereas too much sun gives a scorched earth. Earth without air chokes out all growth, whereas too much air results in a dust storm. Water on the fire puts it out. Fire under a pot of water can make "tea for two." And so it would be with all elements — to be well balanced we need some of each one, in its proper time and place. Nothing is indispensable; everything has its purpose.

It's the knowing how much and how to use it that needs all your conscious mind. The challenge of life which should make it so exhilarating is that every moment we have to make a decision that can make or break us. No matter what task we know we must do for peace of mind, it is our *own* thoughts or decisions about it that save us or "kill" us.

Since it is impossible for us to attend to all elements at once, we attract to us or seek out others that will be our necessary "other selves." The jet plane cannot take the landing field with it so it will be completely independent. There may be wives who can travel with their salesman husbands all the time, but mostly they should not. Two people in the same dishpan only confuse the issue. A son who has airy ideas chooses a mother who will see that he's nourished physically as well as spiritually and a father who will keep him "grounded" or down to earth until he knows his instrument panel.

Again notice any two elements when associated with each other and you'll get an idea on how best to put them through their "paces" for their best performance.

AIR and WATER: Fizz water, sparkling water, foam, a mist, fog, good for washing out and drying, aerated water. Air in the water pipes. "Fish out of water."

AIR and FIRE: Can't live without each other. "Hot air," hurricane, tornado. Fire out of control with too much air.

AIR and EARTH: Well turned earth, dust storm. Packed earth when too little air. Smothered.

EARTH and FIRE: Warm earth of summer, spring, fall, a growing season; scorched earth. Or can douse fire with earth.

EARTH and WATER: A beautiful lake if each in its place, otherwise muddy water or mud, or clay for sculpture. Watered earth productive, if too much, erosion.

WATER and FIRE: Separated by a pot, can be a cup of tea. Water on fire sputters, a wet blanket. Fire boils water over which puts fire out. If gentle — lovely warm water. To a fireman water is a cool drink.

Our irritations mostly come when we don't recognize the good that is in these divergent people or elements. When we are the best in what we are good for, we bring out the best in those we contact, and they with us. If everybody "kept up with the Joneses" we would look like a flock of sheep.

We all need each other to be well rounded, and we have to choose how much and when in order to achieve a more perfect effect.

Also, to be well balanced each person needs play, rest, sleep, creative work, and food. If you persist in overdoing or not doing any of these for a prolonged length of time, you are thrown off balance. If you are tired or pained in any part of the body and you *have not* over-exercised it, then you will know that some part of your thinking may not be balanced.

The Subconscious Is Your Slave

Thoughts, fears, all emotions send messages from the conscious mind through the sympathetic nervous system and the body prepares to act out the request, even that unconscious request, like wishing not to go and finding your car (or body) stalling.

The subconscious, like the earth, knows only to reproduce what is planted in it. If these thoughts are imagined fears or unhealthy emotions of hate, envy, greed, guilt, or resentment, and even if these were "planted" in dreams when sleeping, the body secretions prepare for action because of the unconscious message and you wake up with ailments, the unused secretions for action having become a "poison" in the part of the body that would have acted out the desire or that is the symbol of the thought.

There are people who have so tensed their body for bad news that a telephone call sets their heart to pounding; they have prepared themselves for failure, sickness, and loss of loved ones. "The fearful die a thousand deaths, the brave but one." When you live under tension for things that *may* happen, you are physically so exhausted that you can't cope with the normal tasks or emergencies that *do* happen. The wise traveler crosses a bridge when he arrives at it.

We know that disease and pain are indications of a need for or oversupply of something. We need heat, but too much heat when we draw too close would leave a burn and pain. We are attempting to keep ourselves balanced, but our judgment is not always good. We have within us all that we will ever need for our own purposes and we can use it rightly or wastefully. We have the potential of every disease and every ease. We have around us and within us the tuberculosis germ and every other germ for other diseases, and we "catch" it or give it power when we make ourselves receptive to it. "As a man thinketh in his heart, so is he." If you think you "catch" cold by getting your feet wet or sitting in a draft, you will. But if you take a bath, including your feet — that is different; or being out in the breeze with one you love doesn't count either. Your subconscious mind will reproduce whatever you ask for *and has no sense of humor,* so don't "kid" with it. It is like a dial telephone. The telephone does not care what number you call; it will get the number you dial, and if you have dialed a wrong digit, you have no one to blame but yourself.

There must be a logical reason why, at a picnic of one hundred people, one dozen get poisoned by eating what everyone eats. Or why, during overexposure to the elements, some take "colds" and others don't. Why some very protected individuals have colds continually and others not protected, don't. "There is nothing good or bad but thinking has made it so," said Shakespeare. Not the thinking after the deed but the thinking before you did it. If you continue to think of diseases and crimes you are headed where it is found, as a doctor and a policeman or as a patient and prisoner. One is thinking constructively, the other destructively.

If we were made creative by the Divine Creator in His imagination and likeness, then *we* must be in charge of us. Subject, of course, to the laws of the universe, such as gravity, et cetera, "We are the masters of our fate, we are the captains of our soul." I again say "We" meaning our mind and soul — Body and Spirit. "Christ in me the hope of glory."

We have within us all the power of the universe that we can use, and it behooves us to learn to use it so that it benefits us and is not a means of self-destruction. "Let that mind be in you that was in Christ Jesus."

The disease of any part of the body manifests itself when the soul's purpose and normal use of that part of the body is frustrated. You point your forefinger at "who" is frustrating you; but, if you will notice, the other three fingers are pointing at you, and the thumb is trying to indicate the upward, higher path that can overcome all your problems.

Right Side of Body "Thinks" Male

Who but a man would believe that man is right and therefore a woman must be left? This belief started with a man called Adam. Adam was made from all the things of earth; dust, water, air, and warmth (fire). All the heavenly things entered him when he was spiritualized by the breath of God. He was perfect, complete, all RIGHT. When things are perfect you can't improve them, but — it has to be tidied and cleaned, etc. Perfection stymies creativeness.

God knew that to split a perfect anything would make a magnet that would attract itself to itself, would create a lifetime search, and within each would be heartache and joy but rarely boredom.

God had already commanded the earth and water to create and nourish, populating the world. So most of the receptive, intuitive, patient and cooling water and earth was given to woman. Most of the fire and air was left in man. Fire and air must be free to move around, must not be smothered, and hot air can really take off.

Only a little of the hot-air element was given to woman so she'd stay down to earth, patiently train the children, and be home when that fire and air man is ready for the landing field.

But clever creative woman — she can take the little hot air she has and with that reservoir of creativeness she can increase all the masculine qualities of life she has. But man has not (at the time this goes to press) been able to reproduce himself without her. And no human being can be complete without that right and left side of the body and you can see that on many people one side is the dominant side.

In all great literature, including the Bible, all written by men, we believe, the right side of anything is believed to be the favorite place. The ancient Almanac still divides the Grand Man of the Universe and the Seasons into male and female months of thirty or so days and spring starts with the male (fire). The male signs are air and fire, the female, earth and water. Male is positive pole, female is negative pole. Male and female sandwiched between each other; that's what make the earth and seasons really spin as the earth makes a complete 360 degrees every 24 hours.

Because this right-left thinking has gone on so long it is imbedded in the emotional body (probably even of animals). Thus, if any human is at "outs" with the feminine nature of the world his consciousness pricks his left side with pain or an ailment, and if with the masculine world, then it would be hurting on the right side, inside or outside, top to toe. (This can stop as soon as you know what you are doing to yourself.)

The fact that the masculine side of the brain activates the left or feminine side of the body, and vice versa, is to be expected — they always will. Now if woman brags that the heart is on the left side and the "good liver" on the man side, remember the spleen is on the woman side.

The "middle of the road" types can have middle of the body ailments from center top to center bottom, or on one or other of the duplicate parts of the body as the eyes, ears, arms, legs, and kidneys plus a few other double inside parts.

HEAD

Now we are ready to explain the frustrated thinking that is behind your special pain or disease. The logical place to start looking at the body is at the head. People who have head ailments are potential *heads* of groups, organizations, family, et cetera, and think they are not able for some reason to carry out their ideas. They make plans which seem to them good, and someone else countermands them. Those who make plans and are allowed to work them out to their fulfillment, without undue criticism or handicaps, have no "bother" with the head, but if you feel like a puppet manipulated by another, your ego (I) suffers and you lose "face" in your world. The tension which manifests as simple or migraine headaches, sinus, eyestrain, hay fever, asthma, is calling for attention. At the same time, if you get attention when you weren't prepared for it and you didn't appear to the best advantage, it creates the small illnesses. The more perfect you want a thing to be, the greater can be the headache. Dr. Karen Horney said "perfectionism is a widespread American illness."

When any deep-set complex or frustration was bred into one by the parents, these frustrations created before birth are harder to uproot. If you will remember that although your parents created your original physical body, just as General Motors may have built your car, you are its owner now and it's up to you to control it or remake it. "Call no man on earth your father" for there is only one Father, one Cause, and that is your heavenly Spirit. It is within you for instant use. As the flower is within the seed, so the Perfect You is already within you waiting for unfolding. It has been said that man is both the marble and the sculptor, and he cannot make himself without suffering as he chisels off unwanted chunks that mar the beauty of the perfected vision.

If that vision be the perfection of Christ then even the smallest flaw must be removed and the longer we put it off the more pain. So when you recognize that the flaw is a hindrance to the good that you are doing, remove it.

Many are frustrated and ill because their idea of perfection is of things pertaining to this earth alone. If it's something "you can't take with you" don't let it be a pain to you. There is no security in *anything* that you can see, taste, smell, hear, or feel.

To lessen tension say to yourself, "My body is renewed cell by cell every year. I am in the position of authority that I have made for myself by my present knowledge, experience and personality. When I am equipped for more authority, I will get it. I am filling a place that no one else can fill as well as I and I must not look down on me, *as people in general will have the same opinion of me as I have of myself.* I will not dominate anyone else, or obtain my goods unfairly as there is always a place for real leaders. Love is the key that opens the door to where the keys to every other opportunity are kept. This is love as God loves, letting others make mistakes without criticism. Say, "As I judge others, I am judged; as I love others, I am loved. *The circumstances I am in contain a spiritual lesson for me and I will learn its message."*

Your personality is mirrored in your face. Your body adjusts to carry the head in the way you think of yourself. The man happy with himself and his world stands and walks as he thinks of himself. The face blushes, glows, burns, gets bumps and rashes according to the emotional state until you learn to control yourself.

The eyes (I's) are the ego. Many people feel they must submerge the "ego" to "stay in business." People who belittle themselves or carry their humbleness to the extreme, or feel they have unpopular jobs may have more eye trouble, according to a research group.

The farsighted and the nearsighted persons have different ideas of ego and how it should be compensated. The nearsighted person lives more for the here and now, as to dress, finances, et cetera, while the farsighted one foregoes expenditures of transient pleasures for accumulations that make for security and pleasures of the future. The nearsighted want to do "things" now and properly. The farsighted will wait and procrastinate.

A change in viewpoint has been known to balance or switch the near- and far-visioned people.

It has been said that the right side of the body represents the inherited male thought complex and the left side the female complex. We could say our two eyes are our built-in "mother-father" relationship, or woman-man relationship. If the emotional natures of the parents are so very different, or we could say "they do not see eye to eye with each other," the sensitive embryo records it, and the young child may find it difficult to focus the eyes correctly later. Through love and devotion to the child by both parents, he can outgrow the handicap; otherwise, surgery is resorted to which corrects the physical defect, but the complex may remain. If your "hurt" is on the right side it may have been triggered by man, yourself if you're male, left side if by woman.

I know of a young man who had an astigmatism in one eye. He was constantly unbalanced by his parents' difference of opinion. The day the father died the astigmatism disappeared.

An inexperienced driver is not allowed to drive when he comes to narrow roads. The father thinks the daughter is not sufficiently skilled to drive under these trying conditions and takes the wheel; the daughter gets a headache.   A married daughter feels a lack of authority when the perfectionist mother visits and gets a headache. Actors not given leading parts, when that was their desire, get headaches, or men in business kept in subordinate positions when they want to advance get headaches, or women in groups who are not "listened to" as people of authority get headaches. Women have twice as many headaches as men. So who do they think is the Head?

I knew a woman who for years ran a higher than normal temperature. Tests showed no reason or ailment. A friend reminded her that she was always saying, "That burns me up." When she changed it to "Bless you," her temperature remained normal. The hot-headed type of person can run a high temperature suddenly for no seeming reason. Outwardly he may seem very "cool-headed," but the frustrations, like steam, build up and blow off in the high temperature.

The pimples on the adolescent's face are caused mostly because he considers himself mature enough to make the decisions, but his parents and teachers don't think so. He doesn't dare give voice to his irritation and it breaks forth on the face. If it were from other causes, why should it be mostly or just on the face or affect all adolescents? The passion for sweets is a compensation for the love and appreciation they would rather have from their elders or friends.

Is the flaw on your nose because you are looking down your nose at someone else or because you fear another is looking down his nose at you? I had a friend who had a "spot" on her nose that *must* be removed. It would have left a scar. Two weeks after changing her emotional pattern the lump had disappeared. "If thou canst believe, *all* things are possible."

Still another example is: A man makes all the important decisions of the household, and his wife has the headaches. A wife should be "queen" of the house, or she is a queen nowhere. Even if she makes mistakes in decorations, she stays at home the most and will learn if the "boss" is patient.

Asthma, although a respiratory complaint, stems from unbalanced use of the ego and shows through the head. The asthmatic one may be dependent on a person or a situation and is afraid to break away, but wants to control or dominate. Children who are asthmatic are potential leaders and independent thinkers. They "chafe at the bit" at having to remain in subjection to parental authority. Going away to school usually cures.

Parents should discuss with such a child several possible right decisions and tell the child that it *is* wise enough to decide which would be best, and let the child exercise his or her judgment. Then no jeers from the parent should follow if the child makes a mistake. Everyone makes mistakes; it's a shame to have to have asthma with them.

Because the incidence of asthma is high in very little children, it appears to be hereditary. It is bred into children by the emotional makeup of the parents during pregnancy. The mother may have felt like the asthmatic during pregnancy. When the child becomes mature enough to think and act on his own thoughts, he can overcome it. An asthma sufferer is "out of step" or harmony with his environment. He may think he's ahead of it and is held back by slow "mortals," or "others" refuse to attribute to him the high place he thinks due him, or he forces himself to do things he really doesn't want to do to prove something to somebody he doesn't like.

Asthma sufferers are full of ideas to "get ahead," but they are fearful of pushing ahead against opposition in case they shouldn't succeed. They have not learned free expression and respiration with their fellow men, and the breathing in and out which should be normal becomes more and more inhibited until in extreme cases the breath stops altogether. Breath is the spirit of God without which one cannot live even for a few minutes. As you breathe in and out, know that you are thus "knit" with God's spirit. Do not inhibit it with un-Godlike thoughts. Breath and Spirit come from the same root word.

Asthma and hay fever sufferers compete for love from parents and are sometimes jealous of their attention to the sisters and brothers. In one case, when there were no sisters and brothers and the child had hay fever, there was a feeling of frustration *because* he *was* an only child. If you want to be frustrated you can always find an outside "reason."

In a recent survey there was expressed amazement that blind people were less tense in the business world than those who had no obvious handicap. The reason is clear. The blind person *already* has a physical excuse if he does not succeed. Others not handicapped feel that they must build ulcers, heart conditions, backaches, et cetera, to ease them out of situations their conscious minds won't let them "back out of." God's ordered universe is balanced and one is supposed to rest as well as labor.

You say, "My body is healthy, but my world is topsy-turvy."

There are people who seem to have a perfectly healthy body; but their outside affairs are in a muddle, and there *seems* to be no reason for attracting these problems. Their outside problems are their scapegoats, and they release the pressures that others bury inside. Better to have a flat tire than a ruptured appendix.

Some people feel that it is necessary to blow off steam; but controlled steam in anything, you or your boiler, is the most efficient when it doesn't blow, but is directed into proper channels. The same amount of energy that destroys the furniture could have been used to build a new piece.

To think that boys get rid of destructive tendencies by hurling bricks at an old car has no basis. It only makes it easier to hurl one at any other car. When you consistently "picture out" something in your mind you are creating the reality. Punching bags, yes, and sports, but not destroying things as a game.

People who desire to be the head, or the leader, may 'acquire" a scar by "accident" to their head at the time of frustration and thus may not have the headaches, fever, et cetera. One experience could relieve the other. As a matter of fact, you may already have little scars on your body to remind you of the "over-tender spots" of your past thinking and feeling. They are also marks of your special abilities. Those strong emotional thoughts could have been stepping stones but you stumbled over them and became scarred.

Don't forget that your strengths and weaknesses are one and the same, but differ in degree of application. The roast on the fire is good up to a certain point — after that it's over-done, or burnt. To be "in tune with the Universe" will relieve much of the stress of your life. There is a time for everything — to laugh, to cry, to get up, to go to bed, to eat, and to fast. A person who slept for twenty-four hours at a stretch and then stayed awake for twenty-four hours would find his life somewhat complicated. If you go on daylight saving time when your area has remained on "sun" time, you will miss many dinners, as well as buses. Attune yourself to the speed that gives you the green "go" lights, instead of the red "stop" lights. On the other hand, if others don't march to your "tune" it could be they're listening to their own "transistor." Everyone must listen to his own inner voice and we must let them be themselves.

Many individuals seem to express their ego and their own personality only through shocking and unwarranted action which is out of relation to the group. Sometimes this is necessary. We have to have pioneers in most experiences, but is your action in that category?

MOUTH, THROAT, VOICE, JAWS, NECK

The mouth of a baby is the first part that gets into the action directed by its desires. The first cry tells its world that he has arrived and is in communication; he is saying, "I am." Then comes the sucking motion expressing "I want," "Give me." and he attaches himself to his mother's breast like a leech to obtain his needs. For months and years he thinks of his mother as a part of himself. When she satisfies his needs, he coos; if not, he cries. He wants her with him and may be unhappy when she's out of sight. He expresses his moods and desires by the sounds that come from his throat and a good mother learns what he's "saying."

Before long he wants to add objects to his possessions and, as if all his possessions should be incorporated into his body, he puts everything into his mouth. The mouth is the beginning of the desire to acquire and the canal ends as a place of refuse. This alimentary canal is thus always linked with ideas of getting, repelling, using, hoarding, or throwing away.

Thus our throat, mouth, neck, and voice are symbolically linked with our ideas of possessions, beginning with food. We literally "sing for our supper," day after day after day.

The "head" makes the decision and voice expresses it audibly. The throat and neck motivate the act. If the action we expected is accomplished, these parts of the body are happy.

The place of the mouth in the scheme of life is to receive new ideas, analyze them by breaking them down into small bits and testing by tongue as to quality and taste and, in case nose was off sticking itself into another's business, to note its fragrance. The teeth chew the fat as well as the lean and all this analyzing should go on behind closed lips. The lips are opened only after the ideas are to be swallowed or rejected. If lips open and blab secrets too soon the boss chaps and roughens them up. Lips are not made for gossip. Throat, gums, teeth get sore or loose or boil at being rushed or by delays from head man or others that waste money. One doesn't want to swallow what cannot be paid for. When the footings of the bank account are weak and both ends don't meet easily there's "foot-in-mouth" trouble.

If you have swallowed an idea and put your money in it, and realize you got a rotten deal, your teeth will accept that suggestion, too. You determine never again to bite off more than you can chew and to chew the small print before you swallow.

"The fathers have eaten sour grapes and the children's teeth are set on edge." Every child needs to bite off and chew his own idea after he's on adult food in other things. Same with other members of the family who want to masticate all ideas for the other till they lose their fascination. Very few like to rehash the day's experiences to others in the family, because they may suggest going back and doing it over. Forcing ideas to be swallowed without self-analysis chokes or creates a choking sensation.

Examples of Emotionally-Induced Pains of Neck and Throat and Mouth

I have known children to lose a dime or their gloves for which they paid their own money, and it frustrated them so that they woke up the next morning with a sore throat or a stiff neck.

Older people with property hard to move or sell complain of similar stiffness and soreness.

If it's words that must be said or sung under tension or words said that should not have been said, it could be laryngitis or sore throat, or blisters in the mouth or on the tongue.

Lips and kisses are symbols of love and to withhold words of love or voice words of criticism to those who love can result in dry, parched or cracked lips. To button your lips to kind words, results in the buttoned look on your lips.

Man does not live by "bread" alone which man uses as material or visible wealth, but by every word do we create. "My Word shall not return unto me void." "By your words are you saved and by your words are you condemned!" There *is* power in the spoken word. Be careful what you say. Even "idle" words reveal a thought behind them and some thoughts are dynamite. Don't say "He makes me sick." "That just kills me." Even as you utter it you sound sick and weaker. "I could kill you." "You're a pain in the neck." Don't even think it.

Another example of a throat ailment and its cause. A young preacher forgot his promise to go to a country congregation and talk to them, along with other ministers. When he remembered, it was too late to go; and as he continued his Saturday yard mowing, he mused as to what reason he could possibly give for his absence. Within the hour a lump in his throat became evident. He wondered if it could be cancer and how long it had been there; and if it *were* cancer, how could he go on preaching. His thoughts, filled with fears of loss of profession, loss of income, family privations, et cetera, increased the size of the lump and when he went into the house to speak to his wife, his voice was only a whisper. He could barely swallow his lunch. After lunch he went into town to buy groceries and, fortunately, saw one of the older retired ministers who had been at the meeting. He whispered that he was sorry to have missed the meeting; that his throat would have prevented speech.

The old minister said it was good he had not come and wasted his time, because there were three ministers and only two in the congregation. By the time he arrived home with the groceries, the lump and hoarseness had vanished.

Don't forget — the subconscious will provide you with an answer, a cushion so your "fall" won't be so hard. "Ask and it shall be given unto you," so be careful what you ask. Don't just dial any old number; dial what you really want.

Having to speak to an audience under a handicap of space and acoustics can give one a "cough." Other examples are these: a woman was told to make a call to an acquaintance and she did not wish to; she got laryngitis which cleared up only after she made the call. Another one got laryngitis when she was put on a telephone committee against her will. Still another got laryngitis before her vocal concert when she felt she was not in good voice. Another got a congested throat because she was before a group that asked questions and she feared she wouldn't know the answers.

If you must talk, even over the phone, about a tense money problem, your throat wants to "cough it up."

Many a person has said, "Yes, I was thinking that way but it didn't really bother me enough to cause *this* physical pain." To a very sensitive person, as to a tightrope walker, a "little" unbalance can spell disaster. In a violin a slight turn of the key destroys the melody. Much is expected of those who know the truth of their being. It is our conscience (the consciousness of perfection) that punishes us when we are in error. Thus perfectionist types of people have more tension. Everyone is a perfectionist about something which to another type of perfectionist is very silly.

Sometimes you are about to tell a person something and you aren't sure you should; and you start coughing. Perhaps you'd better *not* tell it. If you cough when you think of buying something, perhaps you shouldn't buy it.

A young child was made to leave her favorite toys at home when the family went on an extended trip. She was not the obvious rebellious type so she "ran" a very high fever and had a very sore throat.

Fortunately, time is the great healer and when our anger has been expressed, the disease runs its course and we seem well again. In some, the scars of the hurt remain sensitive, and they can build up to later chronic ailments unless the person comes to know the true way to think about his experiences. A millionaire said, "When I was four and we were very poor my mother took me to a circus. I wanted a red balloon more than anything in the world, but my mother said it would cost a nickel and would only break, but it seemed that my heart was the thing that broke when I couldn't have it. Now I could buy every balloon that's ever been made and — *I don't want one.*"

An 80-year-old lady said, "When I was first married, I wanted a thin china tea set but my husband said that things like that were not for the likes of us. Five years ago, before he died, he bought the loveliest set of thin china I've ever seen. It sits idle up there on the top shelf. All my friends I wanted to sip tea with have gone. I can't bear to look at it."

These people allowed a little hurt to embitter a life which must have been full of many other wonderful experiences.

If feelings of loss or poverty constrict your throat and stiffen your neck, turn from that feeling to the consciousness of what you have that money can't buy: love, friends, breath of life. If you *use* and show appreciation for what you already have, you will get more. Remember when you wanted more food on your plate and mother said, "Eat what you have first." "To him that hath (the consciousness of having) shall be given," and to him who feels he has not, even that which he has he loses.

"Ask, believing you have received and you will receive." "Before you ask, I have answered."

All that we can use is what we are now conscious of having and we have within us all we will ever need as we need it. "What do you have in your hand?" "Start right where you are." If you pray for rain take your umbrella. A nine-year-old would be wasting emotion wanting a strapless evening dress. When she has something to hold it up she can have it.

It is said that if all the monies in the world were divided equally among everyone, within a few weeks the ones who have it now would have it again, and those who don't have it now would again not have it.

Don't let the fear of losing your purse be so acute that you do lose it; don't have to say, as Job did, "That which I have feared has come upon me." Any thought propelled with emotion has the power to create the thing itself. However, your fears have little effect on another attracting misfortune unless he or she knows about them and incorporates them into his thinking, thus making it his own creation. But there are people who "pick up" your thoughts.

Remember that irritated thinking in any department of your outer world spills over to the other phases of the same "department" *if* it does not affect your body, such as: if you become annoyed with someone who upsets the beauty or orderliness of your home and you break (accidentally?) a beloved object that made the home lovely.

Another example of how wrong thinking boomerangs is when you have fearful thoughts of not having cash to pay bills and it paralyzes you so that you can't think of the things you *can* do to earn more money. Take your focus of attention off the problem and put it on the idea of the perfection desired. "Keep your eyes upon the doughnut and not upon the hole."

NERVOUS SYSTEM,

ARMS, CHEST, LUNGS

BREATHING APPARATUS

Our bodies are symbols of invisible force and intelligence motivated by the conscious and the unconscious. When a child is born, it already has built-in emotional potentials from the inheritance and from the mother's emotions and desires during those nine months.

The environment it is born into plays on those built-in emotional patterns. Think of the child's emotional pattern as the prickles on the circular record which is slipped into the music bos. The "prickles" (experiences, average problems) on the circular spool within the box are the same for all the records. However, each individual's "spool" picks out a different tune from the experiences because his "prickles" (loves and irritations) have a different pattern.

Dr. Ralph Banay, a noted psychiatrist, says it is the home environment that is the prime shaper of the personality. (Personality means the mask you show to the world.)

If the first reaction of a child to an experience in his world is unpleasant, there is a tendency to weave a pattern of dis-ease concerning it. It "settles" on the parts of the body that are symbolical of that emotional thought. That first impression is a thousand times more inedible on his ego than any that come later, thus are harder to erase.

36

The head and throat, I have explained, are the ego and the possessiveness symbols. The head and neck, as a physical part of the body, cannot move far into its environment. Head "thinks," voice gives orders, but neither could participate in actions of the world. Physically they both are handicapped without the action of the rest of the body.

At the beginning, the child thought all things he saw and felt were but an extension of himself. A cry or sound and "they" moved to do his bidding. Then he began to use his arms and hands to reach, touch, grab, hold and draw to him. He was happy until he found there were things his eyes beheld that were beyond his reach. Then he had to cooperate with those close by in order to obtain, and he found there were things he mustn't have and people who didn't always listen to him. He found, too, that the people who could give him pleasure could also give him displeasure; that all those people he wanted to use and possess also wanted to use and possess him; that some of them he was unhappy with but couldn't live without; that you are possessed by your possessions; that all "things" that could give him pleasure have the potential of giving him pain; that he loved the things he hated and hated the things he loved. He was destructive and constructive, social and anti-social, screaming and smiling in a matter of minutes as he tried to control his close-by environment. The "psychology" he experiments with may make him The Boss. This part of his world he could use *without* being able to walk. So his arms, shoulders, chest, his breathing of the air of his close-by world became a symbol of the close relatives, and later neighbors, cars (and the roads necessary), newspapers, magazines, TV, radio, telephones, any printed matter. These were extensions of himself into that close-by world. Breath is a constant contact with our close-by world, so sometimes he would refuse to breathe if he couldn't have his way with his world.

So the condition of these upper parts of the body shows what you think of those things and people who are close to you and your emotional connections with your immediate outer world, as to the type of neighborhood you live in.

Frustrations or lack of harmony with any of these has an effect to the degree that the inharmonious thought is indulged in. If you feel limited or are trying to limit "them," you will have congestion or stiffness or numbness. If you are angry, you can have fever or break or burn yourself. The more unloved or uncreative you feel with all, the more critical the malady becomes. How could you think you were not creative when you see the havoc you've created?

A cold is a combination of helplessness and suppressed anger and creates congestion and inflammation. A cold is an inner "crying" over something you feel you can't do anything about, but you are angry because you can't. If a wife cried in public, someone would think her husband beat her. So — we have colds and can wipe our noses and eyes without explaining the emotion. Even asthma and hay fever sufferers are relieved when they cry but they are usually too proud to do so. (Asthma and hay fever are discussed under "Head.") Dr. Flanders Dunbar suggests that asthma may be a substitute for weeping. Henry Mandalay wrote, "The sorrow that has no vent in tears can make other organs weep."

Medical science is continuing to discover drugs, hormones, et cetera, that can be given or injected to recover the balance your body needs. However, your body will build a resistance to "outside" balancers, because the emotional nature is desiring an "excuse" ; and if one does not balance oneself from within, then, although you are cured of one ailment, another will break out. It is not wrong to obtain a balancer temporarily, but when a person "Comes to himself" he will return to the Perfect Creature, the "Father Within." You *have* a built-in balance wheel. Use it.

After wars it seems the letdown of fighting a "neighboring" nation creates a relaxing into a mass "hate" for that "neighbor" who has caused such waste of men and money, and the coming back of the boys and refitting them into the neighborhood again is very difficult. The results are epidemics, and even the name, like "Asian flu," shows where the hate is directed. We think the boys bring back the germs, but it is the sight of the boys, or the fact that some of the boys didn't return, that renews the hate.

They say that colds are caused by hundreds of different viruses and that they can never vaccinate one against all of them. Thank goodness, if they take away the common cold how can we have a few days' rest and catch up with ourselves? "Germs" and "viruses" do not cause colds any more than cockroaches cause the kitchen to be unclean. Remove the bits of food the bugs have come for and they will go away. The germs are just "the scavengers who must reduce the dead cells back to their natural chemical element." Researchers have put the "live cold virus" on the tongues of volunteers and only those who had an emotional problem took a cold. Never take a cold from another; they needed it or they wouldn't have it. They can keep it as long as it serves its purpose or as long as they think they are supposed to have it — a two-day or seven-day virus. I had a dilly of a cold for ten minutes one day until I realized it wasn't convenient at that time to have it. I had a party coming up. But when I want one I can have it for several days.

But — go on and play your game of viruses. It's such a simple explanation and at the grocery stores we don't have time to tell of the hurts and frustrations that have built up until we "cry" publicly. Then look at the problem as if it were solvable and solve it. If it's really "spilled milk" you are crying over and you cannot un-spill it, then forget it. Why is it really necessary to be sick to have "sick leave"? If all employees were given "well leave" every month it could be taken when pressures had built up to the breaking point and they could enjoy the day off.

The common cold in Mecklenburg County, North Carolina, costs $600,00 per year, and it is said to cost three billion per year in the United States. Vacation money just went to bed.

Researchers found that United States male citizens who were born abroad run a higher risk of lung cancer than native-born Americans. Could it be that the longing for their old environment and relatives or inadequate news about the homeland centered the cancer in that part of the body? After World War I cancer of lungs increased from 1.1 to 11.3 per 100,000; in the ten years during and after World War II it increased 144 per cent. We are no longer isolated. *They,* the whole world, are our neighbors. We were "safer" before our transportation and communication inventions joined us in "One World."

Researchers found that in the polar expeditions when the men were long isolated from the outer world, they were relatively free from colds, but when new men and supplies were brought in, there were outbreaks of respiratory diseases. They contended that germs were brought in, but since there were always a few colds, they could have contracted the "germs" at any time. It is more likely that the messages, letters, newspapers, and the information they learned stirred up their old emotions of the conflicts and fears they had left behind.

During the war a young army wife returned to her lonely room with all the symptoms of "flu." A long distance call from her husband came, and he told her it would be their last few days together before overseas duty and to please come as quickly as possible. She quickly packed and caught the bus. The "flu," forgotten, really flew, and she was not bothered by any symptoms of a cold while away.

A very spiritual-minded doctor advises this to cure a respiration difficulty before it gets hold on you: Breathe in deeply with the thought of breathing in love from the whole world and particularly from those of previous mistrust. Then as you let the breath out, send your love to everyone. If you really mean it, it works. It isn't easy. We have been conditioned to be sure someone thinks ill of us and it is not easy to think everyone can think well of us. And it is so easy to feel sorry for ourselves.

The spirit of man is the breath of you which you can see on cold days. That breath is God within, which never leaves you except to become your invisible Spirit. God is *in* everything that he created. He said, "I will never leave you," and he said this for all people.

In the opinion of James Clark Maloney, M.D., fear is the most dangerous contagion in the world. He has discovered the tensions of parents are transmitted to mentally and physically *healthy* children, depriving them of their normally relaxed condition. If these tensions continue, they make for unbalance in the child or adult.

If you become upset during the day, don't be surprised if your children return from school with a cold or stomach ache. Parents who quarrel even out of hearing should not be surprised if their child wakes up sick, or gets hurt.

This is an example of what a parent's emotion can do to her child. A woman had a relative who wanted her to take a long trip with her. She didn't want to go but she had no real reason for not going. She said she would see how her two-year-old child was when he awoke from his nap. He awakened with a temperature of 103 degrees and the sniffles. The relative went on the trip without her. She called me and I explained how her emotions and desire for an excuse had been picked up. She changed her thought and within an hour the child's temperature was normal and there was no sign of cold. Children will reflect the thoughts of those who have them in charge until such time as they *will* to use their own minds. I am not advising a person not to go to a doctor when something seems to be wrong, but a check into the emotion of the one closest to the child can be a help in the solution. What is the nursemaid's personality? The food likes and dislikes of the ones closest to the child can form his own likes and dislikes.

A woman "developed" a paralyzed arm for three months because she could not tell a neighbor to stop coming over at inconvenient times and invading the family privacy. No organic reason could be found for this trouble. The husband explained to all unwanted visitors that the doctor had ordered his wife to rest and that she must not be disturbed. When her privacy was restored, the normal use of her arm returned.

When we are in our home (our "Castle"), we can be peaceful and good and a "right guy," but it's "those others" that get us down. The associations between people, the closeness of houses, the intrusion of the world's opinions and problems through television, radio, and newspapers into our hitherto private world give us no time to commune with ourselves and those we love most. We "go to pieces." Collect yourself and say, "There is a great stabilizer within every cell, and it is God." If I am running away from a problem by getting sick, I am creating a bigger problem. God or Good asks that you live a balanced life. You are not supposed to be a doormat or a "scapegoat." Create some privacy that even your children must respect.

Say, "I have chosen to live in this world, which is naturally filled with problems to be solved; and if I will calm myself, my world will quiet down." The "flipover" may not be in your "viewer," but in yourself. Say, "I am forever undisturbed." Say, "This too will pass." Everything always "comes to pass" but you hold on to it as if it came to stay.

Do you realize how much you really *like* problems? There is no feeling of accomplishment if you just do easy things. Children make up games that do things the hard way just for the fun of it — like three-legged races or swinging on a jungle gym with arms as monkeys would. When your pushbutton, air-conditioned house gets too easy to manage, you have "cook-outs" with all their "bother." You build beach, lake, or mountain houses and struggle with water problems and old-fashioned stoves and mismatched furniture. This world seems to be the place to solve problems and to overcome something, to test our creativeness and our ingenuity; and when we can't make and solve problems our own way, we have nervous breakdowns or get sick. Remember the commercial, "But, Mother, I want to do it *my* way!" And we laughed — hoping the idea got across to our family.

The space program gets its propulsion from people who were bored with trying to solve these petty, earthy problems which man seemed bent on complicating by not learning from his past mistakes. They would rather conquer new worlds than patch up this old one.

You have often heard that "fences make good neighbors." But a fence is a barrier, and a barrier is an invitation to selfishness and false pride and thus wars.

I once had a dog who was most peaceful and sociable when she was at liberty with other dogs. But let her be protected by a fence or screen door or be in a car, and she would act most vicious and mean, snarling and baring her teeth.

We think we have risen above the level of the animal. We know with our rational mind there are no longer any fences that can separate the peoples of this world. We "talk" of one world, one people, the brotherhood of man, but it is a theory we expound for the other fellow. We want other countries' barriers removed, but *we* keep up our own wall of prejudice and snobbery in our own community and in our own country.

How can we expect whole nations to be friendly when it is difficult to be so with a group of so-called congenial people for two days before there is a flare-up of ego or pride?

The lines that are drawn literally in Europe and Asia and Africa and the United States are magnified from the ones drawn by you and me. The unrest of the world is created by people like you and me and if you "draw lines" of distrust where you are, each line is magnified and vibrated through the world.

It is said by scientists that everything said or thought is still vibrating in the universe and does so until the end of time. You literally have put into orbit around this world every good thought and every belligerent thought you have ever had. Is it any wonder the world is so jittery?

The "Book of Remembrance" is what you have recorded in your own body, your own glands, your own consciousness. Every thought and experience you've ever had, and every deep thought and experience of your mother during her pregnancy with you, is recorded in every cell. Raise it into your conscious mind and either keep it or throw it away. You really can, you know!

One day, when I had *no* time to spare, I had to repeat directions patiently over the telephone to a young girl who was not trying to understand. As I remained calm on the outside, seething on the inside, my respiratory tract became completely inflamed. I had to excuse myself and get tissues. After I hung up the receiver, I gave myself several reasons why I did not have time to have a cold. I also forgave myself for losing my "internal" temper. Within ten minutes the "cold" was gone.

When you find yourself getting congested, weed out the unpleasant emotion and fill the void immediately with a constructive way to look at the same problem. Every problem is a wonderful lesson.

One does not prevent a cold by saying, "I will not take a cold. *The subconscious has no sense of humor and only knows to produce commands* of action and the seed planted is, "Take a cold." Say to yourself, "This experience came to me to test my emotional maturity. I forgive myself for acting otherwise. Next time I'll be on my guard."

Don't plant "cold seeds" in your children. A mother told me her two-year-old girl had slipped out of bed one cold afternoon and played outdoors with only thin pajamas protecting her. When she found her, she scolded her promptly and told her she would take a cold. She did. The next day's paper carried an account of another little child who had wandered away from her home and was not found until the next day. She was also thinly clad and the night was bitter cold. She was found by the patrol and rushed to the hospital for observation. Her mother arrived after she was bedded down and warm, and was told the child had no ill effects from the exposure, not even a cold. The child in the first instance figured that since she had disobeyed in leaving the bed, the least she could do was to take the cold her mother told her she would have.

In my early youth I was told that when I got my feet wet and chilly, I would take a cold, and I did. Later, when I knew that my subconscious would create for me my conscious thought, I played a different tune. When I get rained on and cold, as I love to do in the mountains, I say, "Rain and cold are God's good gift to man, and I will not use them wrongly." Then I do not take a cold.

Be the master of your body; do not let it be the slave of all the wrong opinions of the world as well as yourself.

It is admitted that indisposition has its uses. It is said that Prime Minister Gladstone would get a cold and "take to his bed" when he was scheduled to speak at meetings which could become politically embarrassing.

If a "cold" prevents us from making a fool of ourselves in our own mind, then "catch one"; but know it for what it is and retain it no longer than necessary.

Unbalanced thinking in any section of related things in your affairs can upset the equilibrium of the other things. For instance, if you are upset about a problem in your close-by environment, such as relatives, neighbors, roads, et cetera, it can be taken out on each other or by your car, TV, or your mail getting fouled up. You've known days like that. I'm not suggesting that your TV and your car "fight" but that your tension and frustration affect them. I wonder if, when you are introverted about a problem, it is more likely to affect your body inside, where you think you can have it unseen, or if you want the world to be conscious of your problem (an extroverted thought) it would be expressed where it will show on outer body or material world. As you wait for your boiling car radiator to cool, calm yourself, learn your "lesson"; perhaps you were not in tune with your "good" and the delay is a protection. Bless all your so-called problems and you will be blessed by them. There is good in everything if you will see it.

In any emergency, do not panic. Many a child was gotten well quickly when the distraught parent has stopped concentrating on the problem and visualized the solution. This is the way Christ healed. He did not dwell on the mistake, the sin, the disease. He said that what He did we could do *if we believed* we could.

To stress the good is not the general way of thinking. Parents and loved ones are ready with their "don'ts" and criticisms. They concentrate on the child's weakness and he gets weaker or worse. You tell him he's stupid and then he can't think; you call him clumsy and he remains so; you nickname him "Fatso," and his every bite goes to blubber.

We publicize the unwanted conditions and they get bigger. Our town tried to make *one* day an "accident-free" day; and the newspapers, television, and radio saw that everyone knew about it. One minute after that designated day began, the "free" accidents started and — bang! bang! bang! — they continued for twenty-four hours. The city had never had more accidents; there were between thirty and forty accidents and probably some were not reported. Even little old ladies who had never had an accident got involved in one because they were so afraid they would be the one to upset the perfect day. If you don't want people to think of Grant's Tomb, or children to put beans up their noses, then don't mention it or even think of it.

The Bible tells us, "Whatsoever is beautiful and true — think on these things." Whatever you constantly keep in mind, you become.

A wrecked car on the city square as an idea to prevent wrecks will create more wrecks; the newspaper accounts of criminals and horrors create more of the same. We protest. They say we must tell the truth and face facts. It's a *fact* that more people are good and happy, but it's not news.

Another thought: Could you unconsciously stiffen or paralyze or calcify your shoulders to keep from being "elbowed out" or not have to shoulder a responsibility or unpleasant task? Or was the work of your arms unappreciated? Arms, hands, respiratory system represent communication and transportation, and so does the nervous system.

*

God is in charge of our Spirit, for it is his Spirit, too. God is in charge of our souls, for they are His Children. But He gave us charge of our bodies. When we make Him the head of that, too, then all things are possible.

When a soul is born it comes from His light into the darkness of materialism, and it cries. When the soul leaves the body and returns to that Light, there is a smile on its face.

HANDS

Although the hands are a part of the section including Arms, Hands are so wonderful and intricate and expressive that I will discuss them further under a separate heading. We'll see what "finger" you put on whom!

The hands, fingers and thumb, must work together, as brothers and sisters and neighbors should. They are not exactly alike, and their purposes and functions are different.

For instance, they say that the thumb is the most important member of the hand. It expresses will power, and at the base of it is the mount of love. The thumb can do very few jobs alone, but must bend its "will" with love to the other fingers for real accomplishment. If that love is a selfish or animal love, there is sickness in the thumb. Or is another's stronger will hurting *your* thumb? A woman's relative borrowed her car and the fear she might misuse it stiffened her thumb for three days. When she realized why it became normal in three minutes.

The forefinger is the most likely to point out your best way. We could say it's the "Judge" finger and many forefingers get cut, or smashed, or stiff or pained when one is pointing out figuratively the mistakes of others. Remember that if you're pointing out the mistakes of others, the other three fingers are pointing at you and the thumb is pointing to a higher Path.

The middle finger is the longest finger and represents those who have been in the world the longest. The *middle* stands

48

between the past and the future and is the now; duties we must do *now*. Sometimes we feel that those old people or duties are blocks to our future instead of stepping stones. The present could not have existed without the past and there is no future without the present. Learn lessons from the older ones; do not ignore them or belittle them. Their purposes are not your purposes. *Tend to your own business* and let them do things their way.

The ring finger represents those who wear the "gold crown of authority" in their manner or thinking. They hold their heads high, no matter how "wrong" they might be or how many "mistakes" they make. "The show must go on." However, there are times *we* also want that authority, and we take it and come up against another who "betters" us or has the "last word." Our feelings are hurt that another person acts as if we should not be listened to. We hurt the "ring" finger and it relieves our tension or gets attention in another way. If this thought goes on constantly, that finger may have a chronic malady or constant pain, as an arthritic finger. The ring finger is the "marriage" finger.

It has been noted that the ring finger is the most likely to curl inward as one gets older. Is this to curtail the activities of loved ones?

The little finger seems more free to move around and is rather independent of the others, and may represent that type of person to you. It doesn't seem to have so much practical use and another finger *could* do its work, but it balances the hand and makes it more beautiful. Like the old colored woman who "made" the living, said the beloved lazy husband made life worth living. This finger could represent a person who is your brother.

If you hurt a finger, immediately amuse yourself about what type of person you were unhappy about, or "Who is the matter with you."

Nine years of research at the University of Cincinnati College of Medicine finds that soaps and detergents were *not* the cause of eczema and dermatitis of the hands. Emotion is the trigger and the clenched fist is just one of the expressions of our hands that show our thoughts. Does it "bother" your hands when things are given to us as if it were a "handout"? We speak of having "cold feet" when we are hesitant about walking into something. Could habitual cold hands in a person denote that the owner hesitates to circulate among neighbors and does not particularly like to travel? Poor circulation? Reticent with strangers?

Our hands are our most obviously creative parts of the body and can accomplish the most intricate dictates of the mind. Nervousness or calmness expresses itself through the hands more easily and expresses the misuse or lack of use of the creative principle.

The arms and hands are very closely related to the subconscious mind. Work with the hands "plows" the "fertile soil" of the subconscious mind so it can produce the seed sown by the conscious mind. Those who work out with the hands the ideas of their own minds are more calm within themselves. Even the rubbing of a smooth stone, the touchstone, *is* a good therapy. It is both exercise and a reminder of a desire for smoothness and quietness. To "doodle" while you are listening to another talk lets you "express" yourself without interrupting the speaker. The design could reveal your thoughts about the person or conversation. The hands, as a visible part of our communication system, are used by a speaker to get his ideas across. Some people have such expressive hands they don't need to say much. And some people express so much with their hands that they wouldn't be able to talk if you tied their hands behind them.

Sculptors, painters, poets, photographers have portrayed the hands of young and old, the healing hands, the praying hands. The magnetism in the hands cannot hide your thoughts as they touch, and children especially both love and fear the touch of the hand of the parent or teacher.

The reward and punishment symbol of the hands points out the fact that every thing used wrongly can be caused to curse even though it was made to bless. The "laying on of the hands" to heal. "Don't lay your hands on me" to punish. Many little children spank their own hand as if it could do something they don't want it to. Adults continue this by hurting the hand with an accident or "sickness."

Hands were made to serve with love, to hold but gently, to give and to receive graciously.

The smaller the bones, and the more outside the main body, the more active they seem and the more they can respond to creative thoughts.

There is not another hand in the whole world that is just like your hand, and if you're not letting it do what it wants to do it cries, because there's a little empty spot in this whole Creation.

As your hand can be manipulated so well by yourself, it can also be used by another. "Lend me a hand." "Be my feet today." (Legs also are outside the main body and, as hands, can be hired and fired by the Boss). And thus undesirable manipulation by another body can affect your arms and legs.

Boomerang
Remember, what you give, you get. What you sow, you reap! Everything is a boomerang. Everything returns to its source. It has been noted that the inventors of instruments of pain and torture and death have been in most cases tortured or have died by their own inventions. You *always* get back more than you give but it is not always welcomed.

Have Faith
Everyone has enough faith and if you're not happy with the results note how you have directed it. Do you have more faith

in sickness than health, in lack than wealth? — You create what you think about — think health, think abundance, then live as if you have it, in the face of all circumstances.

"Little men are damaged by misfortunes but great men rise above them and become greater."

LEGS AND HIPS

Arms and legs should work in harmony, and the action of one can have a reflex action on the other. If you have your arms immobilized, it is difficult to walk or run. The legs are able to take us farther and faster than any other part of the body. Thus our long trips, long-range plans for neighbors, relatives, and in-laws, our philosophy and our ideas of religion, all foreign affairs, and books come under the body symbol of legs and the hips. People who write and publish books, write television and radio scripts, or even those who appear on their programs, under stress, may feel a tenseness in the hips or thighs or legs and all muscles, blood vessels, bones, and nerves thereof. For instance a salesman, reluctant to travel constantly, has unexplained pains in his legs. Another instance: A woman had said for twenty years that, as soon as her last child was on its own, she would travel. As the time approached she got leg ailments; she didn't really want to leave home. Erase from your mind *any* picture that is destructive; you *are* in command of your own body. I read of a middle-aged woman who was gradually losing the use of her limbs. It was found that she had been strongly impressed in her childhood by seeing a beloved friend of fifty-five confined to a wheelchair and had built a vision of being in the same situation. Although apparently forgotten, the picture had etched quite a groove in the woman's subconscious; and when she reached fifty-five, her limbs started stiffening. In a few weeks after her understanding of what she was doing to herself, she regained her energy and was soon resuming her normal activities with limber limbs.

Nature always seems to prepare its creatures with the equipment they will need for whatever they will desire to do. Is it possible that tall people with longer legs travel more naturally and with less tension than shorter types? If so, would they also have less frustration in writing or broadcasting, or have less frustration with in-laws? Could it be that, when short-legged people consistently travel, it is for business reasons rather than a natural pleasure? There are always exceptions, of course, but there may be enough truth to make it an interesting study of comparison. Try it!

As arms and legs work in unison, so our ideas of our own relatives should allow similar feeling concerning our marriage partner's relatives.

An acquaintance of mine had a siege of hay fever. I asked her if she had a relative or even a relative of her husband's that she didn't like. She said she did, and although she only thought of her occasionally, she didn't enjoy her thoughts. I told her to love or at least to understand the relative's point of view and it would clear up her hay fever. "But," she said, "I've had hay fever for three years." She continued, "I don't dislike her enough to suffer like this twice a year." So she forgave herself and thought of the relative-in-law with understanding, and the hay fever "went away."
"went away."

I know another woman who had a small rash on her hip every time her husband went out of town.

Blocks in the nerves and blood vessels of the legs are extensively discussed under "Heart and Circulation." If you are trying to block somebody or something either to or from you, you can put blocks in the circulation system.

Medical science has many names for the reasons the blocks are there, as cholesterol or hardening, but they do not know why the same diet causes it in some people and not in others. In a certain mining town where the diet habits tended to create obesity the average adult weighed between two to three hundred pounds, yet there was practically no circulatory trouble or heart trouble. But it was noted that they were a happy, tension-free people and the state of the world or even the country did not overly concern them.

As the world seems to be today it is fortunate that we have many who have dedicated themselves to improving it. But the One who created the world is still in charge of it and needs our cooperation in letting Him work through us. If we did there would be no damaging tension. A water pipe has trouble when there is too much force or a block is placed in it.

Fat in "Spots"

Why can fat just go to certain parts of the body? Could it be that you think too much about whatever that part of the body is a symbol of? Your legs take you further and faster than any other part of the body (physically speaking). If you are a frustrated world traveler — do you have plump legs? Pad your bank account instead of your legs. Your (primitive) legs thought you were going to walk around the world. Now, talk to "them" as you would a puppy and tell them you will take taxis and jets and will not need that fat.

A British-born researcher, whose name was not given, found that smart girls have smart looking legs, that heavy and well-shaped legs means you're sure of yourself and know what it's all about. Bow legs — obstinate; thin ankles — blessed with a sense of humor. You check it out.

STOMACH, BREASTS

The stomach is the home of the food; it represents not only the physical food, but the mental food. Home is the place we take things of a personal nature and from there use or distribute to others as *we* desire.

The master and mistress of the home are the parents, and when there is peace and security within the home, and with the parents, there is peace in the stomach. If a man's *home* life is not happy, his business can suffer. If his business suffers, this jeopardizes the home's security which, in turn, can also create ulcers and stomach ailments. If business failed and he had no reason for leaving home every morning he could be "stuck" doing womanly chores. To most men a home is the place to take off from.

Those who are susceptible to ulcers or stomach aches have a great need to be loved and secure, and a great need to be successful in business to justify being loved. The soft food an ulcer patient eats reminds him of the soft food of babyhood and early mother love before he had to compete in the outer world with the rough "dog eat dog" attitude in business. Now he can't even eat a hot dog.

If your ideas of home and the parent-children relationship in the home reveal incompatibility, then the different foods that come together will seem incompatible. If you will use the time you would spend searching for compatible foods in weeding out your personality quirks that are upsetting the home, you will save both pain and money, and, of course, be a healthier and nicer person. Those allergic to milk may have a "mother" complex. Milk was the first need from the mother and to be truly independent from the mother your body refuses milk.

Vomiting is a result of wishing to return to a situation before "this" happened; then you would handle the incident differently.* I had a dog that vomited repeatedly if her sleeping quarters were moved to another location. A child "upchucking," and thereby excused from school, may be expressing a wish to "return" to a previous experience in school so she could have done it differently. Feelings such as "I should have studied," "I shouldn't have done or said that."

The breasts also represent the home and mother. Baby's first need of home was satisfied at the mother's breasts. When you sought peace from your hurts, you ran home and were held close to her breasts. A woman's feelings concerning love and motherhood and home are conveyed by and to her breasts; and if there are frustrations there, that part of the body is affected. A woman's *frustrated* desire for growth through home or children can easily grow tumors in the breasts (or uterus, the earliest home of the baby). If the desires are not expressed in the outer world, the body can express vicariously the desire for growth, creation, and expansion. False pregnancy can be caused by fear of or desire for pregnancy.

In *Reader's Digest* (July, 1965) in an article called "New Clues to the Mystery of Cancer," by Clark and Deutick, there was what they called an unexplained relationship between a woman's childbearing life and her chance of breast cancer. A woman who breast fed her children a total of 36 months, or

---

* This is the observation of Dr. Harold Wolff in *Stress and Disease.* Springfield, Ill: Charles C. Thomas. 1953.

whose menstruation stopped early in life, had only half the risk of breast cancer.

It is possible that the closeness of the mother-child relationship of the feeding period showed the affection of the mother for children, and the early stoppage of menstruation would have taken away her fears of having too many children.

The report went on to say that they found the risk for *single* women and nuns at least two-thirds greater.

There are women who long for children but are afraid of marriage and the yearning expresses through the mother symbol.

The report also said that daughters and sisters of breast-cancer victims seem to be more susceptible.

Again I point out that whatever you love or fear and hold in your mind your body can express. Better a dagger unsheathed on our person than some of the thoughts that are literally killing us.

Many a woman having children, having a home, still is not satisfied and wants to add a room, or have a larger house, or redecorate. However, she is thwarted by someone or by lack of money. The stomach trouble or tumor she must have "cut out" may cost her as much as the redecorating job. If these frustrations are associated with hate, jealousy, resentment which is "eating her up," or if she feels someone is *"eating her out of house and home,"* then she must quickly change her emotion in order to prevent "delinquent" cells from going completely berserk. People have been healed of all manner of diseases suddenly when they have changed their attitude from resentment to love and understanding. Remember to forgive yourself also. If God is quick to forgive you why can't you do likewise? If you can't forgive yourself then don't pray "forgive us as we forgive" or you are asking God not to forgive you, and you will get what you ask for.

What a wonderful assurance this can give when the statistics of the world scare us with the enormous increase in the "killers." Each day newspapers, television, and radio tell us new things to fear and run from. It takes a great soul not to be brainwashed by it and insist on seeing God (good) in everyone and everything. Nobody but you can separate you from your good.

Read John 5:19-24. No one is judging us but our consciousness of ourselves as the sons of the Father. It is the Father within, our divinity, our realizing that we have done less than the best, our shame that His likeness in us is so badly used or not used at all, "I am my judge and my jury." I am (the human) that *I am* (the divine), the son of the Father. "Be ye perfect as the Father is perfect." How could we even dream of perfection if there was not in us the same potential to perfection that is the Father.

Since the Father judgeth no one (verse 22), but is given the Son to judge and Jesus, the Christ, did not judge even the harlot, and we are told not to judge others, then that leaves only the perfect Me to judge the human me.

What you can *see* (see with your spiritual self) your Father doing (in your body and your affairs) you can do likewise. If you cannot *see* that He is healing you then He can't heal you. He's not a dictator, you know. Of course you need to believe that we are sons of the *Father* as Jesus said.

Many of you readers will say you know people with terrible diseases who are good, calm, steady people, and you are right. Many have chosen to take on personally the "aches and pains" of others. Everyone has a right to choose what he shall feel and think how he shall pass from this world. We know this is only an earthly sojourn of our eternal life. It is not ours to judge and criticize, ours only to love and understand. But many who are young, and have much to live for, are led to believe their case is hopeless and do not know that something their own soul is sick about is killing them.

No one can constantly hate, or fear, or envy, and be healthy. No matter how great the fault of another, your fault of hating is worse. Forgive him — not seven times, but seventy times seven — for your own sake, body, mind and soul.

Many comparatively young men have died of cancer or even other minor ailments who had such great plans to live for, but it is possible to accomplish a great deal of good even in the way we leave this physical life. Glenn Clark has said that he had known people who had tried to do many wonderful things for the world but were locked by people and things. When they had gone from the physical plane, it seemed those same opposing people changed and accomplished for them the very things they had been against. Jesus said, "Because I go to the Father, you will be able to do many wonderful things, but as long as you lean on Me and look to Me for these things, you will not realize your own power." And "You can do greater things than I have done."

As the stomach is the "melting pot" of food, so our country is the melting pot of many homes and many stomachs. We call it Our Homeland. Those who have charge of our homeland problems of security, and those who fear that the insecurity of our homeland might destroy their own businesses, can let the emotion react on their stomachs.

Let those with tender stomachs meditate on the words of Jesus. *"If I live in you and you in Me,* you can ask what you will and it shall be done." Jesus said also we should prove God, that He would give to us so lavishly that there would not be barns enough to hold the abundance that could be ours, and, "Ask, believing that you have received, and you will receive."

We are like a clock which has all the "works" to make it run. Desire is the key that winds it. Love gives it its rhythm. The good desires we have are God within propelling us towards our goal and good. However, we halt and turn away. "It's too good to be true," we say, as we stand in sight of our promised land. We let ourselves be beggars in a land of plenty, "starving at

our own filled table." "All the Father hath is thine." Just ask,
in His nature (name). Prayer is to condition us to receive that
which was prepared for us from our beginning. Someone has
said that Desire makes the mold into which the world will pour
the cast. Be careful what you desire because, if persisted in, you
will get it.

Don't use your stomach as an emergency pantry.

Researchers have come up with very interesting data on
obesity (just plain fat) and its relation to your income and what
"society" you fit into.

They found that, if you have a low income and don't feel at
ease among those of higher income, you are seven times more
likely to become overweight.

This seems to be a case where, if you are not sure of
tomorrow's supply, you overeat today, and tomorrow you do
the same, and so on. In a way you're like the camel who stores
in his body the needs for the long trek through the desert of
privations. He never "goes"; he only "loads up."

Also, if you are lonesome and need more love and
consideration, you raid the refrigerator to "prove" you really
do have what you need.

If families would not be "close-mouthed," withholding
sweet words for each other, there would be less opening of the
mouth for material sweets. Many mothers find it easier to
express their love to the children by lavishing them with sweet
foods.

The chronic refrigerator raider is like a little child searching
for comfort. When you were small and your feelings were hurt
you rushed in crying "Mummy, Mummy," and she took you in
her arms and held you close to her breasts and fed you to take
your mind off your frustration. Perhaps also the rhythm of
the words *refrigeration* and *frustration* play a nice tune in the
stomach muscles.

Cut your food bill in half?

Most people eat too much. If so, eat less. Chew your food

four times as long, making it four times as digestible. Don't buy or eat foods that are so refined there is little food value left. Use daily at least one whole-grain complete food as brown rice or millet or barley (brain food). Use in soups and casserole dishes. You could live on either of these grains for months if necessary. Use nutritious greens, sprout wheat, mung beans or alfalfa seeds. When sprouted, each has four to eight times the food value. (Soak grain overnight, 1 tablespoon alfalfa or 2 of mung beans in a quart jar with cheesecloth stretched over opening. Pour off water and rotate jar so seeds stick to sides. Turn this little "greenhouse" on its side in the dusk for 2 days. Then put in window. Flush with water each day and drain off through cheesecloth. In 3 to 5 days you have a pint or so of greens to mix with foods or eat as salad. Start a jar every two days or so.)

First and last think pleasant thoughts while preparing food, while you're eating and at least an hour after. Bless the food as the nourishment of your body and know it gives what you ask for. Whatever you bless, blesses you. Since your emotional desires direct the calories to where you fear they are going, visualize them instead going to desired places, and the rest, or all if necessary, to energy.

Many people have lost or gained weight (whichever was needed) by eating only brown rice for ten days. To make yourself chew it more, eat it half cooked. Sound nutty? Tastes nutty!

INTESTINAL TRACT

To be well balanced physically and mentally, we must let the foods and ideas that are taken in be assimilated and distributed where needed and where they will do the most good. In the body this is taken care of automatically and naturally if you are at peace with the world.

What we must understand with our conscious mind is that our emotional thinking of *giving back* to our world affects the intestinal tract, so that we can control it when it misbehaves.

The foods seem to say, "Use me but don't abuse me"; "let me work, don't rush me or tell me how," as they proceed from the stomach through the intestines. Those who feel uncomfortable in those regions feel abused, not used; servants, not serving. The things they're given are not being used as ordered, or not appreciated, or not used at all.

Certain types of people have intense compulsions to help others — so much so that they are not always wise in their ways and times of helping. Sometimes their motives stem from a desire to be needed, in order to inflate their ego, or to tie someone to them through duty or obligation. Whatever the motive, if you have indigestion, or a spastic colon, or intestinal "flu," or types of ulcers or other disorders there, it is because you are frantically sorting and shuffling, or pushing ideas or things on people without the proper motives, and getting undesirable results — like the Boy Scout who helps the little old lady across the street when she wishes to continue on the same side of the street and you see your so-called good deed wasted.

The same type of person who is predisposed to intestinal disorders has conflicting ideas between the ego and what he considers the necessities of life, such as food and clothing, and the serving part of the house, such as the kitchen, where the "servant" most often is needed. The people who depend on you for these physical necessities, but will not listen to your mental guidance or suggestions "to the letter," can set your bowels aflame. Even a pet who expects all comforts, but will not obey, can do the same. The irritation outweighs the joy as you fill its bowels at your expense.

At the base of it all is a feeling that you are not really loved and wanted and needed. You begin to feel like a servant or housekeeper, paid or unpaid; a bundle of tools that others use, not the gardener.

The world could not do without this tender intestinal type of people when they are living in their higher consciousness. They are perfect coordinators and organizers and analysts. Their awareness of all the minor details of everything and their sense of the rightness of things makes one confident that he can depend on them to do the proper things for all types of functions, business or social.

Just as all our faults are caused by going overboard with what were good qualities in the beginning, these people "can't see the forest for the trees." They must try to see the total picture and tell themselves that if it isn't going to be important five years from now, why let it be so important today? Happiness in the home and peace in human relationships *is* important, but five years from now will those cigarette ashes on the floor, the socks that don't match ties, or lipstick that doesn't blend with the nail polish be remembered as you live alone, because everyone has left you to be "bossy" by yourself?

If you wanted to grow exceptional flowers, you would study their preferences for sun, soil, water, and food. Are not your friends and your family more important? Are not those people in the office, who are a necessary part of your success, worth a little personal understanding?

When you give, do not feel hurt if it seems unwanted or unused. You are the more blessed because you gave.

Think of the fact that our Maker has placed in this world everything we will ever need. He has given it so tenderly and lovingly, but we are free to take it or reject it, use it or misuse it, and we can have it and keep on having it without even thanking Him. He even gave His perfect Son, that we might learn better. The Son became the people's servant. He was despised and crucified. Still He loves us and gives us His all.

Remember also that when Martha was bustling about, being the proper hostess for Jesus, and Mary sat at His feet to learn of Him and to adore Him, Jesus said Mary had chosen the better part. There's a time for being Martha and a time for being Mary. We must take time to praise and adore those we love. Praise, born of love, is the most healing salve in the world.

Praise yourself also; you cannot successfully love and praise others if you do not love yourself. The second most important commandment was to love our neighbors as ourself, assuming we loved ourselves.

Anything that you give that is not motivated by love does not do your soul any good. Love does not demand anything in return, but because love draws its own to it, those who love *are* loved.

Someone has said that gravity was the earth's love-nature and, thus, always drew earth's creatures back to it.

Colitis

It is the general opinion in medical science and psychiatry that colitis has its roots in the feeling of guilt.* There is a great

---

*Alexis Carrel: *Man the Unknown.*

need to be loved but one may feel unworthy of that love. I know a very young child who did what she later found out was very wrong. She was panic-stricken for fear it would become known to all the neighborhood and she would never live it down. The resulting attack of colitis almost finished her. The guilty want to be punished and illness satisfies that need. The inner skin of the body reacts to your thoughts as does the skin of the external body, but the inner skin is a more hidden and secret thought. Thus colitis-inducing thoughts could be an "unknown-to-the-outside-world" guilt. Introverted types have "inside" ailments more easily while extroverted types prefer illnesses that *show*. Some ailments are very "popular." If a "bug" is going around, they want to be sure to get their share.

Colic, Etc.

Many ailments of very young children can be traced to the parent's emotional condition at the time of the child's illness. The emotional state of the mother when she is carrying the unborn child imprints the body with a susceptible pattern. When the child is stubborn enough and old enough to think for itself, then the pattern can be broken. Remember, every physical cell is renewed every eleven months, but the memory of the soul can be forever. Sometimes a physical predisposition of a body is chosen by the soul because of his life's purpose. Then it must be lifted into the conscious mind, where it can be forgiven and erased if it is something unpleasant. Our soul progresses by overcoming.

Constipation

Constipation expresses a desire to slow up or stop a condition or experience in your outer world or to hold on to people or property or money. A feeling of lack, or poverty, has reflex action in making you hold on to the food you had yesterday for fear you won't get any more or better food tomorrow — but to hold on to things that are no longer useful "poisons" the owner, whether it be food, junk, or old clothes.

See chapter on "Elimination Avenues." Little pockets in the intestinal tract are a way to hold onto material things of yours and hide them from those who may want them.

Diarrhea

Diarrhea is a manifested wish to get a thing over with so as to return to a desired routine or life. Soldiers waiting to go into battle are plagued with diarrhea. They desire to get the whole thing over with.* Some people have a desire to be rid of a duty or obligation to somebody. Others desire to get something over with, as a visit which you don't expect to be pleasant.

If a child under your care is bothered with these above conditions check into your own thoughts, too. Some children are always rushing "things," others hold back. In **zone therapy it is suggested that the heels be massaged while you chat with "him." This relaxes the muscle in that region. Massage the rest of the foot while you're at it for general body tone. Read under "feet," for understanding. (See the printed zone therapy chart on page 190).

*

If the nutrients in the blood go to all parts of the body, why can toenails be soft, fingernails hard and hair thin or thick when each is made of the same "stuff"? "Thought in the mind has made us what we are."

*

"He has some gall" means: impudent, to fret or wear away by rubbing, to vex, irritate or harass another. To build gall stones or kidney stones is a way the child in you would collect stones to hit something or someone who irritates you. Forgiving is less painful and expensive.

---

*Harold G. Wolff, M.D., *Stress and Disease.*
**"Zone Therapy," by Wm. H. Fitzgerald, M.D., can be had from Health Research, Box 70, Mokelumne Hill, Calif. 95245.

THE FEELING CENTER: SOLAR PLEXUS

The abdominal brain is the sympathetic nervous system, known as the solar plexus. The twelve solar plexus ganglia are receivers of energy from the back brain and are the "brain" of feeling and sensation, not of thought. The solar plexus broadcasts feeling and sensation to all parts of the body. When your feelings are hurt, the reason and the "who" is indicated by the point on the body responding with pain. Lift it from the feeling center to the higher brain and eliminate the malady by redoing the projected thought.

The solar plexus lies just back of the stomach. Since the feeling nerves are connected also with the stomach, it's easy to see that your stomach pain is more likely to be something you felt deeply emotionally rather than something you ate. It is said to be impossible to think without some emotion.

Since the solar plexus is the distribution and receiving center of feeling, as the intestinal tract is of nutrients, the same type of person who is predisposed to intestinal disorders has the "nerves" of the abdominal brain too aware of too many things. They don't know how to be quiet and relax. We might say they seem to have antennae into the whole world in general and are too "helpful" where help may not be really appreciated. Even though the information could make over the whole world, they must realize they must *love* people, *but* let them progress at their own rate and make their own mistakes. If the antennae are tuned to pick up the good and the beautiful, they will find it; but if they are tuned to see the faults that you may criticize, you will find that also. Your suffering will be your reward and, added to it, *they will criticize you.* Whatever is broadcast is always harvested a hundredfold. You criticize another and a hundred people will think critical thoughts of you. Love and praise, and a hundred people are benefited.

Since one cannot see in another a fault which one is not also capable of, do not reveal your "worser" self by criticizing another. "Let him who is without sin cast the first stone," and when none did, He said, "Neither do I criticize you." Also in Romans 2:1 we read, "Therefore you are inexcusable, O Man, whoever you are, if you judge: for the thing in which you judge another, you condemn yourself, inasmuch as you that judge practice the same things."

*

Very rarely does anyone deliberately want to hurt your feelings. They were blowing up their own self-image and you were the sounding board. Or, they love you and *thought* it would improve you. Everything that comes to us is for the best to mold us into our true divine character so we should not be so stubborn. When we ask that we learn patience and understanding we get the ingredients. Perhaps we didn't really mean it. A person that can change his mind and let *no trace* of the old thought remain, except to be glad it happened, can change the thing in question immediately. "In the twinkling of an *I.*"

Mononucleosis

International experts on study of mononucleosis find the "victims" were pressured, consciously or not, by higher ups beyond what they could or wanted to do. It is *not* infectious and no virus has been found. The healthiest succumb and it can be mild or severe. Students start with depression when facing a crisis without a solution. Those with most motivation to get well quickly did so even in severe cases. Mild cases can drag for months. Young people out of school and on their own for the first time and finding a career or romance hard to handle were susceptible. Experts agreed that the disease was highly over-treated and over-emphasized.

Don't Name Ailment

Don't call your ailment by its fancy medical name; *it* will love you so much you will hate to get rid of it or destroy its image. What if your disease were able to be Prosodemic, or you had Furunculosis, or Gomphiasis. If you could pronounce them, and tell your friends, you'd get a great deal of sympathy. So, unconsciously you hate to let the conditions go. But if you tell them what it means, that you have boils on the skin which is contagious, and your teeth are loose, they are likely to smile and avoid you. Don't you remember that duck you got your children on Easter and they named it Donald? You can't eat it, or kill it, or give it away. It is friend and to you a fiend. So whatever ailment you have when you think of it call it "a thing" and it won't like you well enough to tarry. If you called your neighbor *that* she'd shun you.

*

The cells of the body have the intelligence to know their purpose in life. Nose cells only rebuild noses and ear cells only rebuild ears, though each is fed the same food. So why is it not understandable that one can "talk to and praise" his body and it will respond? Be careful what you impress it with.

If scientists have found a plant can go into an emotional tizzy when a live shrimp is dropped in boiling water, does it not follow that a human's cells are even more responsive and intelligent?

ELIMINATION AVENUES: RECTUM,

KIDNEYS, SKIN, LIVER

Now that we have taken in and used and distributed, we must let go, or throw out, the things we no longer need.

For every bag of groceries we bring in, we have a bag of garbage to throw away. The food center of a household must have constant attendance; one day of neglect and we have a breeding place of parasites.

As the throat represents the good things of life that come to us, such as food, money, negotiable property, so the pores of the skin, the kidneys, liver, and lower alimentary canal represent the use of the bank account and our hoarded assets, or what we inherit from the past, or leave for future welfare. If there are fears or worries, or irritations concerning these things, the colon may become irritated, the blood vessels or muscles are "ordered" to swell or contract, and to try to stop the flow of material assets to unwanted places. Hemorrhoids and constipation are the results.

To hoard through the kidneys causes kidney ailments, infections or building crystal upon crystal until we have stones. Stones, such as gall and kidney stones, are a dignified way to gather stones which you cannot throw. If you were a small boy, you would pick up a stone and "let it go" at whoever "bothers" you and it would not be buried in your system. However, you'd

71

have stones thrown back at you. All in all it's better to forgive them.

To hoard waste that should be discarded naturally through the skin is the most public and obvious manifestation, and it could possibly be linked with the feelings of obstruction and ostracism, which is symbolic of skin irritations. Are you ashamed of your job? Yourself? Or what? The erupting skin is giving you an excuse for withdrawing from people — something to hide behind. The unlovely thoughts you do not wish to express make you feel unhappy around people. The more you are conscious of the pleasures of any part of the body the more likely that *any* frustration with it becomes a major problem or dis-ease.

External organs which perform the passing, or death, of waste material are the givers and receivers of the germ of life, as well as the physical avenue of the new life. What is death but the beginning of a new life? Paul said, "Each day we die." Each day we must throw out wrong ideas, used material, et cetera. Each cell, as it renews itself, must slough off the old. Alexis Carrel kept a chicken heart alive over twenty years by daily renewing the nutrients it needed. Thus it has been proved that we do not die of *old* age. Probably it is an accumulation of old emotions.

There are those who hold on to material assets in an unreasoning way, presumably for their loved ones, and create disorders in these corresponding parts of the body. It is likely that they also have a fearful attitude towards death, their loved ones' or their own, or concerning some inheritance they wish to leave to someone, but are fearful that it will not be distributed rightly or used properly, or they may fear their own inheritance may not be received. Some people are not content to limit people they love (?) while on earth but leave limiting wills that erase all their love for them for years afterwards.

"Take my will and make it thine; it shall be no longer mine."

God's will to you is to give you everything you really want and ask for and He lets you take it to use it as you see fit. Therefore, do not bind yourself to earth by your will and possessions. "Whatsoever thou shall bind on earth shall be bound in heaven; and whatsoever thou shall loose on earth shall be loosed in heaven." (Matthew 16:19)

When we really believe that life is eternal for all people, our bodies will not be bound in binding ailments when our loved ones are on dangerous missions. God is there with him or her and you or he couldn't have a better Protector. Fear within you can bind them so they are not in best form for their work.

Computed Emotions

We have through our lifetime computed into our body different thoughts that are irritating and they are stored in different parts of the body. When a similar thought or problem comes up it seeks its kindred thought patterns, and thus in a given experience participated in by many, the reactions on the bodies are different because the memory banks are filled differently.

We can train our body *not* to act out the dis-ease which does not help the situation at all. If we can stay well while working on a problem we can lick it more quickly — If it's more *time* that is needed to solve the problem, just be a little sick until the time is over. We play "games" all the time. Anyway, this is a beneficial one, and you will be able to laugh at it.

*

"Ye are of God, little children, and have overcome them: because greater is he that is in you, than he that is in the world." 1 John 4:4

HEART, BLOOD VESSELS, CIRCULATION

If we present no interference, nature and our body are forever trying to maintain perfect balance. Even the hurricanes bring the minerals and the elements from the south seas that we must have and could get in no other way. Lightning charges the air we breathe with necessary ions for vitality and mental alertness. Work, play, rest, and sleep balance the body. If you can't take time for resting and playing, then work with every cell in your body, happy and singing — glad to be alive and well. If you don't think you are happy, pretend you are and it will help you to be so. Shakespeare said, "Assume a virtue if you have it not." Replace the thought of things you do not like with a vision of the things you do like, and it recharges your body like a magnet.

Grace Kelly acted out the princess role and so lived the part that she became the Princess of Monaco. The world in general is willing to agree with what you think of yourself; but if you don't do something to back up your thinking, the world mind maintains the balance by bringing you down a notch.

The heartbeat is timed to a person's thinking and the activity the mind calls for, be it real or fancied. Many of man's fears he can control as long as his conscious mind is in command, but fears are buried in the subconscious and in sleep and dreams the subconscious is in command. The ailment you wake up with was not because you breathed night air but "dug up" nightmares.

The heart attacks one has in sleep and the ailments one wakes up with are the results of this misuse of the creative principle. "Thoughts are things." "Mind becomes matter" or "mind is matter" thoughts, words, matter, or flesh.

Before going to sleep, one should surround himself mentally with the love and protection of God's love and turn over all problems to Him. "Pray as if everything depended on God" then next day "work as if everything depended on you."

Pain in any part of the body is like a little dog barking to let us realize we are off the right path. Many people interpret it as the bite of a dog. If the pain is in the big toe or some muscle twitching, we dismiss the fear and the pain goes away. If the pain is in the region of the heart or stomach, it is hitting at one of those vital places that advertisements have warned us about; and before we realize it, we have built a minor tenseness into a major pain. They say there are five million people in the United States who have all the pains of a heart condition, but do not have a heart condition.

On your way to your doctor's office to have a professional checkup to relieve your mind, be probing into your emotional life to see where you have been thinking unloving thoughts. Read First Corinthians, Chapter 13, to see what love really is, because you may have forgotten.

You see, the heart is the body's symbol of the "love" of your life, of the things and the people you love with your whole being. Whom do you love the most? Most people would say they love the marriage partner or the children. Sometimes one says this, but his actions show that he loves only himself. He laments, "I slave overtime for my family, to provide everything they want." At the same time, those he loves would prefer less of the material and more of his presence and attention. If they don't love you without the fur coats and expensive cars, are they worth your "killing" yourself for? You can't buy their love. Don't have to say, "I bought my son everything and he disgraced me." He did not disgrace you; you disgraced yourself when you neglected him in those early years when he thought you were wonderful. You provided for his material needs, but what did you do about his soul yearnings? Don't have to say, "My heart is breaking. I showered my wife with everything any woman should desire and she left me for an ordinary man who will never make a name for himself." She married you because she thought you loved her, not because you had a famous name. You neglected her while your ego concerned itself with glazing *your own name* before the world. You glorified yourself.

The greatest treasure in the world, love, cannot be bought, sold or lost if it is tenderly handled and not neglected.

It is good for those married and those who hope to be married to know that those who truly belong to you can never be taken from you by another. If they are not truly yours, you should not want them. They would never be really yours.

Sometimes it seems love gives us so much trouble that if it were not for love we would have no problems. True! If God had not loved the world, He would not have made man to share it. If God had not loved man, He would not have made Man a co-creator capable of producing his own species and his own individual world, and his own heartaches.

The seat of love, that is to say, the *physical* seat of love, is the heart. It is the center of the circulation system which carries love (blood) to all other parts of the body (or world). To withhold love or affection from someone to whom you feel it should go, puts a block in the blood stream in the part of the body symbolized by the person or thing; the arms, if it's relatives or neighbors, or legs, if it's in-laws or friends, et cetera. (See chapter on that part of the body).

Sometimes the block is there because a person is truly sensitive or tenderhearted or free-hearted and the love he tries to give to his world is misconstrued or blocked by red tape of others.

Sometimes there is a desire to put a "block" up so those of the world cannot get through, and in privacy one can "catch up" with one's self. "The world is too much with us," said Wordsworth. I once had a dear famous friend who said that it seemed man spent the first fifty years of his life trying to get the world to know he existed and the rest of his life trying to regain his privacy. Eisenhower's heart attack was precipitated by irritation at being interrupted by telephone messages unnecessarily when he was playing golf.

Any sudden display of deep emotion, be it anger or love, has a very instant effect on the heart as well as the whole body.

Sometimes a sensitive person is put in a position in business where he must "lay down the law" or dominate situations in a hard-hearted manner. This may be so out of character that his soul is "sick," that right action must be forced on people. Yet he has gotten out on a mental and emotional limb and cannot explain to loved ones that his position in the world is out of character. He had rather land in an oxygen tent than give up any other way. These people literally die for their principles.

You would think that dictators *should* die with a heart attack, but they have no qualms about their "rights" to lay down the law. It's not what you do, but the way you feel about it that causes the stress. Work can cause less damage than trying to get out of work, or working when someone is trying to "make" you rest. Much stress could be spared older parents if they would be allowed to do the things they want to do without the children trying to get them to do nothing. The strong-minded ones do what they want to do anyway, but they have the added burden of "shaking-off" the arguments of those so-called loved ones.

Typical heart patients are usually men of action and they can rarely indulge in the contemplative life. Their attitude toward life is that they had rather "die with their boots on" at the height of their success than see themselves grow old and turn their businesses over to a younger person. Some fear that they would not be loved if they were "old and useless" and the "heart" of life would be gone. To think of retiring into a life of leisure is worse than death to some people. Don't make just *business* the heart of your life or when business is over the heart is gone.

The "blind spot" of many of the worst cardiac patients is that they cannot listen to another's point of view. Their ego acquired for them their place in life that gives them a right to be the *hub* of their world; and when they make a statement, even if it's wrong as they may later find out, their pride makes them stick to it. The hub is of no use without the spokes and outer rim. Don't find that you are a general without an army. A heart attack can give you a chance to withdraw gracefully, to relax and to take the ease you should have taken earlier. Re-evaluate your life and get a fresh start. To keep body and soul together, let the soul and spirit lead the way.

We breed future health conditions in the male from childhood on by saying: "Be a little man"; "Boys don't cry"; "Don't back down"; and "Show them who's boss." They are urged into activities contrary to their gentle nature. There is in every person both the male and female principle. Tenderness and understanding should not be flouted by the male. We are truly mated when we see our best selves mirrored in another; so why do we fight to be different?

It is easy to see why fewer women than men have heart attacks. Women don't have to prove their superiority in the business world; they can always resort to a "a woman's place is in the home." They are like the weakness of flexible steel in comparison to the strength of brittle iron.

A woman also takes more pride in her figure at middle age, or at the middle line. You don't see women pat their "bay windows" with pride. Women also tend to eat what's good for them, while men had rather "eat it if it kills me" if it should be one of their favorite "poisons."

Rheumatic Heart

According to medical findings, rheumatic heart conditions are sometimes contracted by sensitive souls who are shocked at the death of loved ones or the lack of love between those who should have love. Sometimes it is because the patient himself does not love someone whom tradition decrees he should love, such as a parent or sister or brother.

To develop an unborn baby with a healthy heart, see that there is plenty of love and understanding between the parents and for the child to come. The best way to heal a faulty heart is to love, really love its owner. The surgeon may be able to mend a damaged heart, but only we can give it its daily food. The health and education of a child should start before it is conceived.

Blood Pressure

People with high or low blood pressure are those who do not really believe that God can regulate all their affairs, shoulder their responsibilities, carry their burdens. Those with high blood pressure are suppressing inwardly the hostility and rage they feel because someone else or some thing is regulating their affairs and they cannot express themselves any other way without hurting someone they love.

Anemia

Anemic people should walk in the fresh air and breathe in life too seriously and stay tensed for bad news or disaster. Anemia can be caused by constant indecision by those who are afraid to really live by their decisions.

"For the life of the flesh is the blood." Learn to live with joy. Joy is the emotion that draws in oxygen for the blood and makes it pure.

Anemic people should walk in the fresh air and breathe in the oxygen and eat food that gives them the needed iron for attracting elements for red blood cells. And live without fear. "For I have not given you the spirit of fear but of love."

You can eat nourishing food and worry so much you get very little good from it.

Never worry about the mistakes you have made or you only live in the past. "Let the dead past bury the dead." All great people have made mistakes and learned from them. If you've never made mistakes you've never done anything either, so you must be dead. Your soul came to grow and you grow faster if you know how to surmount your learning processes.

What is Divine Love?

"I may be able to speak the languages of men and even of angels, but if I have not love, my speech is no more than a noisy gong or a clanging bell. I may have the gift of inspired preaching; I may have all knowledge and understand all secrets; *'I may have all the faith needed to move mountains* — but if I have not love, I am nothing. I may give away everything I have, and even give up my body to be burned — but if I have not love, it does me no good.

"Love is patient and kind; love is not jealous, or conceited, or proud; love is not ill-mannered, or selfish, or irritable; *love does not keep a record of wrongs;* love is not happy with evil, but is happy with the truth. Love never gives up: its faith, hope, and patience never fail." I Cor. 13 (Good News for Modern Man version)

All Prayers Are Answered

Prayer is a deep desire for or about something and if you persist you will get it, even if you don't want it when you get it and it destroys you. If this happens your answer was not from God and was not good.

If you ask in your prayer to Him for something and say "if this is for my highest good" then you may not get what you wanted, but a better thing you will get even though it may be some time before you are sure. In the meantime you might ask for something that would cause your "highest good" not to come to you and so, He could *not* grant it.

Some prayers have priority, you see. If you "ask for bread can he give you a stone" and break your teeth out? I'm sure glad God *is* within me. If my own personal God was any further away He sure would have trouble keeping tabs on me. I can hardly do it for myself on the physical plane.

*

"Do not fear competition; if you are not pushed out, you'll be pushed up."

ANKLES, ARTERIES, VEINS, BIRTHMARKS

There are many parts of the body that doctors know have reflex action or related symptoms. One is the swelling of the ankles which can be associated with heart trouble. Symbolically, it would seem that the action of the ankles represents the action of universal friendship; thus love that goes beyond kin and neighbors. If the circulation of love from the heart must go to every part, it must send out to all friends and people without thought of gain in kind. The feeling that you are more friendly or have done more for your friends than they for you limits the circulation, and swelling and stiffness and lack of action in the veins of the ankles are the results.

Rushing and worrying to outwit the "adversaries," who would bleed you and take the "fat of the land" from you, impress the arteries and body to store and preserve that fat for you to slow the bleeding. Its name is cholesterol. Tell your body to relax in the knowledge that whatever is yours in the Divine plan will come to you and cannot be blocked by man. You *are* your body's only boss.

Varicose veins are so relaxed that the blood takes longer to return to the heart. Sometimes a person is disturbed and hurt that the love gifts (life's blood) that have been given out are so slow in returning to the giver. The giver is blessed by the giving and though the gift may be slow in returning, it gathers other blessings on its way and when it comes, it comes as a stranger and has increased beyond recognition.

The Creator's good gifts go to all alike with no thought of getting the same thing back. We give because we must. A tree that does not drop last year's leaves and fruit would never bear again and would die.

It could be that the swelling ankles of a pregnant woman are caused more by a feeling that her activity with friends during the last months and after the arrival of the baby will be curtailed. Baby sitters cost money, and perhaps the budget can't be stretched any more.

I know of a pregnant mother who was terribly hurt by the unfriendliness of a close neighbor who did not share watermelons with them, and the pregnant mother was too poor to buy them. Her baby had a large birthmark on her ankle; and, as it grew up, it was so inhibited by her inability to make friends that she was seventeen before she knew what a real friend was.

Edgar Cayce said that a birthmark was a special mark of one's soul on the body to keep reminding him of what he must especially work on in life. If you have a birthmark, read the section on that part of the body and use if those things in your outer world are your complexes, your phobias, your weaknesses; when they could be your strengths.

When a business man marks certain papers for certain uses and it is accomplished, the "mark" is removed. If it does not get done, he makes deeper marks of urgency on them. Birthmarks *do* go away, or they can get more pronounced. "Either finish this or else −," says our soul.

It would be interesting to note what unproductive thinking you are indulging in, when you hurt any part of your body or even "accidentally" break something. Any wrong thinking you do, not just concerning yourself but anybody else or anything else, boomerangs on either your body or your external affairs. You may feel a friend has let you down and you fall because the action of your ankle was not relaxed.

Once two friends were riding in a car but were feeling very unfriendly towards each other and saying so. Gnats bit their ankles until they were raw, although they did not bite a sleeping child who was with them in the car and who did not share their temporary animosity.

I know a retired man who resented the many visits of a friend when he wanted to be alone. When he saw him at the door again, he suppressed his anger and as he opened the door, wishing to turn away the visitor, he turned his ankle and fell, breaking his hip. The hip is the instrument of action of running away, which his soul could not do. He had wished to be alone. He had ample time to be alone in the hospital and nursing home, but at what a cost!

"Agree with (understand) thy adversary quickly, lest a greater ill come upon you." This is never to be interpreted as punishment from God. It is our soul punishing us.

Many times friends disappoint you and irritate you; but if you imagined that you and that friend were the only ones on a desert island, you would really value that presence. Or think of your own shortcomings in being a real friend to someone. The Master, who sees within us the perfection that we could attain, still sees us only in love and waits patiently for us to attain that perfection. "If you will be My people, I will be your God." It's like ourselves in a mirror. "Draw nigh unto Me and I will draw nigh unto you."

Love binds us to the world and to each other, but we have a choice as to whom we will be bound to, both in the visible world and in the invisible spiritual world.

Could this be true of DIABETES?

All ailments are caused by imbalance in the chemistry of the body. This chemistry can be thrown off balance emotionally or by what goes into the body through foods or chemicals, etc.

What triggers diabetes is that the body has not balanced what are called the "sweets of life." It's also called the "gravy" or the icing on the cake.

Life and living is a matter of give and take, and each relaxes or rests the other, but on some the seesaw gets stuck and stays down too long. The yearning for the sweet ideal is overpowering. When they do get it, it still doesn't compensate; a perfectionist is never satisfied.

Many times there are obvious reasons why they think the sweets of life have been taken away from them and the pancreas is impressed by this thought and fails to transform the sweetness from the food. Many older people develop diabetes rapidly after a loved one has passed on.

There is a great increase in diabetes in young people. It could be partly because all processed and bottled foods and drinks used so much are heavy in syrup and sugar. They are also eager that they have all the cultural advantages the wealthy have. A love affair or loss of a loved one can trigger it. Many parents see that their children have a dessert (sweet) when, if the truth were known, they are starved for love and understanding from the parents.

This "starving" for affection could be started prenatally. If so, love is free; better to spoil with loving than suguared food.

Remember that love is a "two-way street" and some think that all sweets should come to them and none be released.

*

Where Do We Get Our GO?

From the fact that everything has a positive-negative polarity. You walk forward and behold one leg is going backward. As the top of the wheel advances the bottom is receding. Even as it starts backward it comes under stress on the road, the tire wears out. That's bad? Then why don't you jack up all four wheels and drive the car? You'd get no wear and you'd get no where.

BACK

The back, vertebrae, muscles, etc., are the "support" of the "head man"; so one's thinking about the ability to support an idea, a project, is symbolized by the back's condition.

The lower back concerns itself with maintaining the balance of the body — so much here, so much there; who does this, who does that; income, outgo — and if one is thrown out of balance, and harmony cannot be maintained, the results are known as backache.

There is the imbalance of power between marriage partners who should be of equal status. Unequal power, even of the heads of state or heads of countries, becomes backaches in sensitive people who bury in their bodies the injustice of the situation. The symbol of justice is the scales to balance the actions of people, as nature endeavors to balance even when man tries to unbalance it. If you think you are balanced *but* you must balance the actions of another for "his own good," your own back suffers.

You could think someone dear to you is too gullible, has no "backbone," so you stiffen your own back to be the back for both. This could cause backache in either or both, whichever is the more concerned over the protection.

Another example: a boy got a back "trouble" when his father refused to fully support him. The father did it to strengthen his "backbone" but he responded by relaxing it altogether.

Sometimes the wish to have things that the bank account cannot support or the necessity of supporting someone you cannot get "off your back" will create a tenseness there. A woman's husband loaned $20.00 to a friend. She said, "We can hardly support ourselves — do we have to support your friends?" The next morning she wakes up with a backache. Some people will not ask for help in carrying the load and yet refuse to "back out of" an undesirable task. Say to yourself, "This is no burden, it is a privilege. Whatever I do in love comes back a hundredfold so I will love and see the spiritual growth; in love my burden is light." As I release the thought that this is a burden, it is no longer a burden; and every muscle, tendon, and vertebra and disc between is now in alignment and is lubricated with joy and love.

The balanced life is also one of giving and getting. A painful back may belong to one who can give but can't graciously accept, or whose conscience hurts him because he receives more than he can give, or his ego hurts because he gives more than he receives.

If two people were walking a tightrope hand in hand, they would have to be in one accord. Marriage should be like that; but sometimes one of the marriage partners starts pulling too much in one direction, like over-spending or talking too much, and the other pulls in the other direction to balance the act. This creates distance between the two. There is an expression that is appropriate: "If you can't lick 'em, join 'em." But Jesus said to *come to an understanding with your opponent, or you are the one who suffers.*

In most cases if you understand a so-called "enemy" you make of him a friend. It is not necessary that all people be close friends, it could be very boring to both parties. Even the types of fish in a large aquarium will mingle with their own kind.

If you have a "backache" try to stop being a perfectionist till it corrects itself. If I had to live with a "Perfectionist" it would "break" my back.

A little imbalance is a lot more fun, like rocking the boat when you're out with the girl friend. The movies end it with the near fall, catching her, and the long kiss.

You can be separated from those you look to for support, mentally or physically, and your back becomes sensitive with the thought.

KNEES. . .BONES IN GENERAL

RHEUMATISM AND ARTHRITIS

Our bones hold us up in the world so we can stand like a human being and not flop like a jellyfish. Our bony frame is the symbol of our standing in the world. We can sometimes get by with acting as a jellyfish in the privacy of our home, but in the outer world it would not suffice. We must hold ourselves up.

To feel that others underrate us, that our pride is hurt, will start the body processes to giving us an excuse for not standing upright; you can call this by several names, such as arthritis, rheumatism, bursitis, backache, etc. When these symptoms start in any little part of the body, note of what that part is a symbol and nip it before it overcomes you. Don't let your body be a bundle of excuses when it was made to be a bundle of divine possibilities. Bursitis in your "writing arm" could be because someone doesn't like what you've written.

One "bends one's knees" to those in authority and if one feels that one wants that authority without kowtowing to another's wishes, then the stiff knee will help you. Forgive yourself for that false pride and the pain goes away. This has been instantaneous many times.

If you have obligated yourself to try for a position of authority, even to the "top of the mountain," and are afraid that if you do get there you might not be able to do all you have said you could, then the pained knees will seem to prevent

89

you from climbing there. One cannot climb one step without bending the knees. What really can prevent one from getting to the top of the mountain is the conviction within that you could not or should not get there.

Falls that occur may be preceded by a fearful mental image of not succeeding; or it could be an interpretation of false pride. You have heard so often, "False pride goeth before a fall."

When we visualize ourselves in a high position, our soul wants us to have arrived honorably and fairly. Start right where you are to work out your true purposes.

Affirm for your soul and give freedom to all others, and you will offset the fear of bondage or lack that stores up wastes in your muscles and joints and bones.

People of rigid will, with strong opinions that cannot change within changing circumstances, find that their joints can more easily become rigid as with arthritis or rheumatism. To try to "push" another or be pushed by another who is opinionated will also stiffen your muscles and joints.

Rid your mind of skepticism and criticism. Lubricate your joints with love; to refuse to do so only hurts yourself.

For your joints' and bones' sake, learn to say, "I'm sorry." Say often "I love you." If you are out of practice, write it to those you love and write it often so that your joints are "oiled." You must give love without binders on it if you are to get back love without being bound in rigidity.

To write or dictate a Will binding another to some hardship can harden your bones into the shape of your rigid will. "I will not be moved" may be the same theme song of those who cannot change with changing circumstances.

We want all 206 bones of our body to work together in harmony, but every bone and every connection between represent vital connections with others outside who are "bone of our bone and flesh of our flesh" and it requires tact and understanding to make even two move as one.

The most important symbols are the head (skull): The head represents, who is the head, first mother-father, then Boss, then I? Vertebrae, ribs, and breastbone represent: I supporting and "thou" helping protect our vital parts of life, physical, spiritual, and emotional. For as the "rib was taken to create thou" she represents the breastplate and shield of the heart of life; she before, I back her. In the business world, it is the partnership that protects and shields each other from all sides.

The pelvis supports the vital parts from the foundation up, I, thou, home, business.

The arms and legs (126 bones to 80) are more in number, and they represent people that are extensions of the main organization but can be hired and fired or borrowed.

The Power of the Subconscious for Healing

Never talk or think despairing thoughts about unconscious (or conscious) sick people. It's worse than hitting them when they're down. Those who love them should keep them surrounded with God's love, then no negative thoughts can get through. Remind them that they *are* loved, that healing power *is* available for all and that God *never condemns or* wants anyone to be sick or suffer. Prayers are more powerful when audible – *but not within hearing of the person.* The person *must* be asleep or unconscious when you are saying it. Call their names 3 times to get their attention.

Louise Eggleston wrote four booklets on the subconscious mind and gives examples of successes (address p. 206). One retarded 6 year old, with damaged brain, could go to public school when he was 9. A 14 year old boy left home for 7 years. His mother talked out loud to him all hours of the day and night, a week later he called and wanted to come home. A young man crazed with grief was committed to a padded cell. In 10 days he was perfectly normal. Rules: 1 "If you can believe *all* things are possible," and 2 "Ask, believing you have received and you will."

Mothers and teachers can help slow or discouraged children. Nurses and doctors can give their parents a more optimistic viewpoint. Some people say they don't want to get another's hopes up. Without hope we "fail" anyway. Even miracles are still happening to those who believe it.

FEET

Your feet represent the foundation of your life, and as such they represent the hidden side of your personality, just as the foundation of a building is hidden but a most important part of the building. Thus, the feet represent your secret hopes and desires, your innermost dreams, waking and sleeping, your fears of limitations, the "skeletons" in your closet, and, in general, the past and the closeted part of your thinking.

Your feet are your under-standing. It is the understanding of the past, both the mistakes and the successes, that determines the present and the future. Whatever the background, do not be ashamed of it but use it. It was the *best* to give *you* your experiences and your present knowledge.

That is something to stand on – something to take off from. "Earth is our home, but heaven is our destination." We rise out of tradition, but are not bound to it. The purest white lilies rise out of murky bogs. We see the miseries of the world, but should not become a part of the misery. We must do what we can to help others out of the mud, but not be pulled into it by them. Say, "I must wear no one's shoes but my own. I fill a place or wear the shoes that no other can fill but me; and if my station is high or low, I will accomplish it with love and understanding. I must love and understand myself if I want to help my fellow man. I *am* forgiven; I must forgive."

Take a pencil and paper and set down the things you have stood for up to now. Now, erase, or cross out, all hate, greed, jealousy, pride (what else is this beautiful pair of ill-fitting shoes that were not made for you?). Purge your mind of those things, those secrets, that have created physical agony. When you have no more emotional torment, your body will be free and whole, and your feet a beautiful foundation of your life.

"How beautiful are the feet of those who bring good tidings" or how uncomfortable are the feet of those who bring or bear bad or unnecessary tidings. One night a woman heard that a friend had reported an incident of her carelessness which she had wanted to be kept hidden. It irked her because there was no need of its being repeated. Her foot became inflamed until she realized that she must forgive the friend, not bury the anger in the "footings of her Temple."

When one is too sensitive and overly sympathetic with the "underdog," the feet are too tender. Talk out your hurts, or write them down and burn it, or cast them on the Great Creative One who says, "If you confess your mistakes, I am quick to forgive." When you go into your closet it is not to cry over your hurts or see the rattling "bones" of old hurts of the pain but to commune with your divine nature.

Before going to sleep each night, consciously say to yourself that the evil thoughts of the world cannot get through the invisible shield of God's love that surrounds you, that only constructive thoughts that teach a lesson will reach you, and that you will learn a lesson from every experience you have.

A girl, unable to sleep, wakes up in the middle of the night, writes a letter to a friend, beginning, "I know you want to kill me because I have not done what you asked me to," and the friend dreamed at the same minute that she *had* killed her. An idle word? Yes, but idly tossed thorn seed comes up better in the flower bed than the carefully sowed petunia seed.

Whatever we think of the other people in this world, we consciously or unconsciously expect them to think of us. If we are suspicious of them and hate them, they can feel no differently about us; because that is the law of the universe.

What we get is what we have given; what we give, we get. This was said 1900 years ago by The Greatest, and it seems so simple and so fair. When you analyze it, it could be no other way, or this material world could not stay in balance. Read Romans 2:1. For wherein thou judgest another, thou condemnest thyself; for thou that judgest doest the same things."

When we are trying to understand other people, we must remember that the road back to Perfection means a different thing to each person. Bless them and let them do it *their own way*. Imagine, if you will, many people in a large forest. Some are where it is dark and filled with bogs and briars, and the way for them is slow. Some are in a clearing and seem to be making much progress, but a swamp looms ahead, and temporarily they are slowed up.

Some are "out of the woods" and have no problems, but they hear the cries of those floundering in the marshes and go back to help them. There are "saints" who take on the problems of the weak, because they know that for that purpose they were born. Our soul knows that the "highest" and the "lowest" people are bound by the one Father within and the highest must share with the lowest, because the lowest is the highest and the highest is the lowest; "the last first and the first last."

Sometimes your feet "insist" on being immobilized for a while, so you can catch up with yourself. There is good in everything. Elevate your feet and get your meditation and reading done. The feet can be used wrongly to sidestep obligations and, though they appear to outsiders to be going somewhere, your soul knows the real truth. The knots or calluses on your feet could be knotty places in your understanding of situations. Work on better understanding, and exercise the feet also. The blood supply that goes through the feet goes to every other part of the body. Since it is far from the heart pumping station, the circulation gets sluggish and deposits crystals. These are warts and corns and calluses. Massage them and let your circulation right itself.

Do not belittle yourself because your dreams of perfection lift you into the clouds and you "awake" to find your feet still earthbound. Dreams do become true realities, and the realities could no more be without the dream than the harvest can be without the planting. The things that grow above the earth are nourished by the earth in the earth.

The feet are the part of body most in contact with the earth and desire a secure footing. It is the desire of most lives to have "roots," as a home of their own, and they do not feel secure unless they have their own place. Since the feet are the meandering part that takes one far from his "roots," then one may be uncomfortable without roots. Either make that secure home for yourself or realize that perhaps for you a home would be a handicap to your true purpose, but whatever you do decide — *stand on it.* Stop shifting from one "stand" to another. Stop always being unhappy because you are not some place else. When Paul wrote, "I have learned that in whatever state I am, there to be content," he was in prison.

The feet are the parts of the body farthest from the heart (love center). Everything of importance seems to reach every other part of the body before it finally gets to the feet. Sometimes people with "unhappy" feet "feel" they are only getting the leftovers, what no one else wanted, or what was going to be thrown away; or that they have to wait a long time for what they want. This upsets the feet. They burn, blister, get corns and calluses or the bones refuse to support the body. You might say the feet are really sorry for themselves and feel they are always being stepped on. They feel martyred.

To have happy feet, look at life this way for them. The feet are the foundation of the body. If you understand life and what it *really* is, you feel good all over; if your understanding is muddled, you feel bad all over. So change the emotional quirks that cause tender feet.

When good things come to you through the arterial blood and through the nerves, don't "hold" them too long before understanding the situation or you create corns and calluses, but send it back as Love, "venous" to blood to all the rest of the world (body).

Disease or pain is sometimes the working out into the open of an undesirable subjective condition. When you recognize the purpose, use it for good and get that fresh start.

A young horsewoman grew a "spur" in her left heel. A girl who rode at the same stable she considered very standoffish, and unkind to the other horses. She thought she was a real heel. I asked her to see if the girl wasn't lonely and unloved. She befriended her and they buried their differences. As the "spur," no longer needed to dig into her enemy, melted away, it left a more mature child.

Do not employ your feet to have your body run away from situations or problems and then have your feet hurt because "they" are to blame. "Take my feet and let them be swift and beautiful for Thee."

"Stand still and see the glory of the Lord (Law)," the law of cause and effect. Understand yourself and accept yourself. Jean Stafford said, when you accept yourself, "It is like falling heir to the house you were born in and have lived in all your life, but to which, 'til now, you did not own the title." Now look at your very own house, your body. It has some faults, but without those some other good qualities could not have been. It may be difficult to live with a perfect person anyway. Now, you are its master and can do with it as you will. Every moment you show your wisdom or lack of wisdom. You gain experience by each decision.

"Be ye transformed by the renewing of the mind." Man is atomic power. You have that power — use it rightly or you disintegrate your world (body). Every cell has in it many atoms. Desire splits the atom into energy. Direct it into your perfected desire patterns.

*

"Let no man say when he is tried, 'I am being tested' by God, for God has nothing to do with evil nor does he try any man. God is absolutely good, and his will for us is good. It is our deflection from his will that causes the evils or trials from which we suffer." James 1:13-17.

*

If you are slapped on the left side (the feminine, receptive side) turn to him the right side, which is the positive, "masculine" God of Love. Thus the cycle is finished with love.

A FEW DANGEROUS THOUGHT SEEDS

Have you planted such thought seeds as these in your subconscious soil? It has no sense of humor and will produce only from the thoughts of action. For instance, it "hears" *take a cold,* not the *don't* you said before it. Erase these thoughts from your mind:

"I lose face when I'm with her." (She deflates me.)
"I closed my eyes to it."
"I didn't want to hear."
"It just burns me up."
"I've bitten off more than I can chew." (Teeth)
"I've bitten off more than I can swallow." (Esophagus.)
"I don't think I should say this." (Cough)
"He'd cut my throat." (Money)
"Cough it up." (Financial, usually.)
"I'd choke first."
"I didn't know which way to turn" (Stiffness)
"Don't crowd me, I can't breathe."
"He gives as if it were a handout."
"I'm empty-handed, useless."
"That's hard to digest."
"I'm fed up."
"I must grow, expand, be more creative." (Vicarious growths.)

"They're eating me out of house and home."

"I must eat while I have it." (Fattening up.)

"Oh my aching back." (In jest?)

"Get off my back."

"My back is to the wall."

"He'd take the shirt off my back."

"I have to *support* his wishes." (Back)

"He won't back down."

"I will not let things move me." (Stiffness)

"I will not bend the knee to him."

"I wouldn't turn a hand for her."

"I will cut him down to my size." (Cuts)

"I was helpless to change the situation." (Temporary paralysis.)

"I didn't want to let. . . . . . go." (Rigidity, constipation.)

"It can't go fast enough." (Diarrhea)

"I mustn't say what I want to, I just let it pile up inside." (Gall or kidney stones, crystals).

"My heart is heavy with grief."

"I'd have to harden my heart to get any rest or privacy."

"He's breaking my heart."

"He'd take my life's blood."

"I play it cool with certain people." (Shy people are subject to poor circulation, as cold feet — cold hands.)

"Don't run out on me." (Legs)

"He's a heel."

"Don't step on my toes."

"They won't support me."

"He let me down." (Falls)

"He pulled the rug from under me." (Falls)

"I'm walking on hot coals." (Self-torture?)

"Turn a deaf ear."

"It took my breath away."

"I smell a rat." (Nauseating ideas.)

"She has a bad taste."

"He hasn't a leg to stand on." (Support inadequate?)

"Flat-footed." (Lack of finesse.)

"She rubs me the wrong way." (Rash, itch.)

"Such gall. She's a bitter pill."

"I feel it in my bones."

"Shoulder responsibility."

"I'll toss my weight around." (Fat)

Hands can "cry" when another won't "lend a hand." (Weeping eczema.) They can burn or itch when you're not "handled" rightly. Clenched fists hold but cannot give, are alerted for self-defense.

What to do? Love and forgive yourself, analyze "Who" by part and condition of malady. Love and forgive them. Or, continue to suffer.

Ways To Diagnose Yourself

If your ailment is emotionally induced you must "know yourself" or you'll never know anyone.

The difference between health and sickness is a misplaced I (ego). Webster says the word *Aliment* means nourishment and the word *Ailment* means pain and illness.

If you put your own I in 3rd place, as I after "You" and "them", and do it willingly, you have your health made better.

Our ego is the cause of most problems. When deflated some part of our body hurts.

Extroverted people have ailments that *show* on the body or that are proper to talk about. Introverted types have inside ailments or on covered parts of the body. For right side or left side ailments read pages 21-22.

If it is down the center of the body from top to big toes where the hurt is, it may be the world situation or a person who is so balanced or unbalanced that you cannot change or shift "it" to suit yourself. The situation is a "middle of the road" complex, unbending, immovable, or so it looks to you. Relax — look at it another way. Our security can be that some things don't shift. "Even a stopped clock is *right* twice a day."

The size and shape of your body reveals what *you* think is of most importance in your life. Even the long and short of it is revealing. For instance, if you are overweight from the hips up what I have listed in this book as their symbols in activities you have over emphasized, or if larger in proportion from the hips down to feet, then read of those activities as most interesting to you. Have a good talk with this childish body of yours and explain "they" were interpreting your thoughts in the wrong way and that fat or pain will not help solve your problem. The long and short shows your divine plan, the condition you have caused.

Now let's look at how the type of physical problem can describe the type of emotion: boiling, burning, scratching, cutting, pressure, helpless, paralyzed, desire to be more as principles, growths, and over secretion. Stiff, unbending, breaks can apply to relationships.

When you know who? Why? What? Ask yourself:

1. Will suffering solve this problem?
2. Will it get me into or out of what I desire or what I didn't want?
3. Is this my only way to make a break, have leisure to reshape my life and start over?
4. Do I really want to live and be well?
5. What lesson, material or spiritual, can I learn through this experience?

Whatever you say to yourself "face" up to the truth. Since your Creator does not condemn you why keep beating yourself as your own "whipping boy." God knew that our human nature when under our will would play games with truth. We play at leaving the Father within because we don't need him; we pretend He isn't there, and then we pretend to search for him everywhere but in ourselves where he has always been. He *is* life; he *is* health. We must stop refusing what he *is* giving us in every breath we draw. (Read pages 152-155).

MY OTHER
THOUGHTS

I APOLOGIZE

Forgive me if I have caused any to have more physical and emotional pain than you already had. It may be an emotional "operation" and it *is* more painful than before. Thus it was with me when I got into this way of thinking. It is like the chaos of spring housecleaning and you promise yourself to thereafter do a little daily and stop piling up things out of sight.

These are my condensed findings of about fifteen years of searching for meanings for me and my understanding of the ways and laws of my Creator.

If they help you it is probably because we were on the same "road." If not, you did not need these same answers.

To many this will be thought to be unorthodox and unscientific, but I feel Jesus and Paul would approve of what I have found. No research lab can take a person and check him against another for proof because no two people are alike and mind can be changed by any person with the speed of light.

In finding certain thoughts behind certain ailments I left "no place for me to hide" either, and I've learned to face myself with my "precious" faults and have learned to love myself in spite of them. I found that God had already been doing it to me, also.

Learn to laugh at your faults and ailments. If you should ask me "who was the matter" when I have ailments, I would say, "Do you want my excuse or my emotional reason?"

Run from problems? You know, if you run away long enough you meet "it" on its "come-around." I confess that I do not like to write, even letters. In spelling I did something to English that has made educators evolve a "new spelling" and they have published a Misspeller's Dictionary, just for me, I'm sure.

These Other Thoughts which follow were the "pictured out" answers to letters which said "You are right, but how do I change my mind about conditions?" I have tried to give you other ways of looking at the same thing. As: For years I looked at a beautiful tree in my yard, and wished that the ugly growth on a high limb could be removed.

On one early dawn it "left" when "it" became a tree nymph. The "growth" was her head, the branch out of it her tossing pony tail, the limb down to the trunk had the contours of her slender shoulders and hips and legs, a limb went from her shoulder to hold on to the trunk. Now every morning I look at the *loveliest* part of the tree, my tree nymph swinging around her maypole, with birds in her hair and on her shoulders.

*

Is the Master your friend? Could you carry on a conversation with Him as you relax with that midmorning cup of coffee? And as you say what you feel do you listen to Him to know how He feels and thinks about you, your problems, life in general? These are questions — you have the answers within you.

Write down the adjectives to describe the type of person you are thinking of when you say, "He thinks he's God." Now — is that what you think God is? If so, in many cases you should change your mind. He is a God of Love, not condemnation, not dictatorial. His laws of "sowing and reaping" are that we will know that justice is being done, and that eventually everyone is paid for everything.

HEAVEN IS ON EARTH

We ask that it be so with very little idea of how it would be and what we would do. We are living in a Spiritual world made of Spirit by Spirit. The ground on which we stand is holy ground. What we would do is what we have done and what we see of heaven it is what we see now. What do you call what you see? Every bit of everything is God "stuff" or is made of "stuff" made by God. There is nothing in heaven or earth that was not made by Him.

He took the glory the heavens "declared" and made it into our earth and all within.

Then WHY doesn't it look heavenly? May I paint an illustration?

You see a lovely mountain scene, everything is in the picture that man needs, everything is where it's supposed to be. It is mirrored on the earth plane in a lake so clear that as above so is it below, the straight trees are straight and there is "heaven" on earth. Since everything is perfect and calm there is really nothing to be done, so we fall asleep.

We're awakened suddenly by the sounds of people and boats. Living, experiencing, learning, people communicating with people, learning to command the element of water and the things man has created that he may walk on a boat on water and rule the waves and air with his body and sails, and to rule the elements of fire and earth.

106

Here's action! This is living! But where has that mirrored heavenly picture gone? It's still there but the more active the life is the more you have to see it in glimpses. In the ups and downs of every wave there's a bit of the above and a bit replaced by things around you and you have to *know* that you are seeing the mountain and sky and trees by the essence of it, by colors on the water, not by its shape. The trunks of those straight tall trees are seen as crooked or even as pieces of its color on water. The way he makes the crooked straight is by Him in us knowing it was as straight as we "saw" it; and as we know it IS straight, it is.

Many have never seen that original heavenly picture except in a desire or a dream or as a promise, because this earth was made for souls who wanted to learn lessons by doing, to be tempted so they could resist, to try to succeed in the face of probable failure. At all times they would be learning to command the things of the universe. They would find that the good things that God had made, when in their own human hands, could be used wrongly. One of the things it was the most difficult to learn is that if it could not have had a negative-positive force in it, it would not have been visible, and if it had not the possibility of being used wrongly it could not have been used rightly.

This negative-positive force is difficult to handle, it troubles and muddies the waters with its mistakes and our glimpse of a heaven state is only dimly seen.

Be still and know and listen, don't talk, and the waters become still and the "picture" comes back. We have to live beyond what the five senses know, to where Love and Truth abide or we would not get even a sample look at perfection. But if you can get one little glimpse of it you know there's more and we can get more the same way we got the sample. The best way to "see" something is to BE it.

To see God, be what He is, Divine Love, Light, and Truth. He is not a dictator, bossy or critical. To be heavenly, try to be all the qualities that God is and consider people more important than things. Be giving of self and praise all that He has made and grow in wisdom and understanding.

So could I live on earth if it were like heaven? Could I try for one day to have no un-Godlike thought or act?

Don't wait for the world to declare a Be Heaven Day. Don't declare it at all; if it's not secret you couldn't do it. All the best things of life are quiet and come in the silence.

You Are Creative

Your thoughts are so creative you create negatively all the things you don't want to happen — and that is because you *think* about them. What gets your attention gets you.

These are thoughts you shouldn't think: "Everytime I'm in the tub or have my hands full, the phone rings." "Don't drop that." "You're going to fall." "You'll be sick." "I burn the food every time I have company." "I can't. . . . ."

To keep people from calling when you are in the tub, *know* that they *will* wait until it's convenient.

When the six children are coming home from school, *"know* that I am the calm eye in the midst of the storm."

James A. Mangan in *The Secret of Perfect Living* (Prentice-Hall, publishers) has given switch-words to be used.

It is like flipping a switch when you want an electric appliance turned on. Conditioning your mind to believe is getting the house wired and the appliance; the rest is almost instantaneous. Then to change any condition think or say CHANGE.

To receive help in transportation, say ON. On, on the light switch, means light and action at the end of the connection. It makes a transportation connection.

If you *have* to do something you feel your body isn't able to, say ADJUST. Like climbing stairs easily, or getting help with chores. COVER is the word for reducing over-excitement.

Many will prefer to use these words. Whatever you give power to will be power for you. Others will prefer to know that "God in me can do anything I need to have done, in the best way, at the best time."

These are just ways to gather your scattered self together into one purpose and belief. *The Magic of Believing for Young People,* by Claude Bristol, is wonderful for one who prefers not to have the Bible quoted.

Sometimes you are feeling that because one little part of you is "sick," all the rest of your parts can't go to the party. It's amazing what happens when you know you can do it and want to.

This belief, this way of thinking, can easily get you parking places, tickets to games, and a thousand and one things per week that you've been getting the hard way.

In a store I found draperies just the right color, etc., and said so, but I wanted them in a longer length. The clerk said, "I'm sorry, these are all I have left." I looked at them and grinned as I said, "Do you think they will get longer if I keep wishing?" He laughed and said it would be a good trick. Then light dawned and he recalled that he believed there were two pair back in the supply room, and there were. "Wishes *are* horses and beggars *can* ride."

How many times I, who am an optimist, drive to a front best place to park and there's a place — all the pessimists didn't even look there and had parked far away.

Create or Suffer

That which is not used spoils. We cannot deep-freeze our creativity. All are creative. It is His creative image in us that is the Son, the spark like the flame of the Father.

This creating was to have been done with some part of your physical body and it will act like a prima donna who is not allowed on the stage, and sulk, or ache, or boil over, and threaten you with more pain if you don't let it perform.

I have just read that creative people in the arts, who are not too frustrated, are noted for their abundant hair. Those who determine to be hard-headed businessmen are not frustrated artists because they are not artists.

Do you think that's why musicians were called "long hairs" and why the "hippies," determined to do and create their own way, choose the long hair?

A person longs to do creative work with her hands and she's so busy with duties she can't. In order not to have "sick hands" she should do it anyway for a few hours a week, or she could realize that down through the ages a woman's hands devoted to duty were more honored. Hands are healing when placed on a sick child's body. Magnetic strength is there when love is there. When you do what you have to do with love, it's "a happy body."

The most obvious sign of unused creativeness is nervousness and thus nervous breakdowns. We can't build hospitals fast enough to contain them. A hobby room would have been less expensive, yet many people think that the home and all its various activities should satisfy the woman, and they let them become increasingly nervous and frustrated and will not see. "There is none so blind as he who will not see." In the end the man may find he has to work extra to pay medical bills because the whole family gets frustrated.

Love and release is the secret to well-being. This is the God way. Any other way is prison and poison.

WEIGHT PROBLEMS

If you are weighing too much try giving yourself away.

Those professional people who "throw their weight around" are proud when they can throw or lift more weight.

Your subconscious sometimes acts like a monkey that understands your every word and does whatever you say even if you were thinking a joke. Remember the missionary in the jungle that preached forgiving by telling his converts to "heap coals of fire on his enemies' heads," and they did.

Read what I have said under the Stomach chapter. Overweight can be because you are insecure and are storing up excess for the lean days, but they never come — and now, what to do about it. (Read pages 61, 62).

"Give us this day our daily food." Now that would really help! It would mean we wouldn't have to refrigerate "store" food that gets bugs in it, have spoilage and fruit flies, locks, theft insurance, pantries, refined foods that are so filled with softeners, extenders, retarders, coloring, etc., that no self-respecting bug would be caught dead on it.

Can Time Be Wasted?

Don't think of changed plans as wasted time or knowledge not needed. Our soul sometimes tricks us into learning something we didn't think we needed or getting a smattering of what we thought would be a career. A student got in wrong (?) lane of traffic and thus to a different university than planned. The Latin course gotten there to fill in was the "peg" his later career was hinged on. Another took prelaw for a year but decided not to be a lawyer. His life work could not have been done without that knowledge of law.

"GOD IN ALL" PICTURED OUT

Make a visual aid to explain "God is all in all" for children of all ages.

Cut out three rows of paper dolls of different colors of comic strip. Put the dolls in a circle in three rows (more if you like). Let the first row be close in to the center, with arms around each other, the next row with hands touching, the next with each separate, arms down.

Stretch over all of it golden (or white) cellophane. You could tie a tiny gold bead in the center so the yellow looks like a sunburst.

The yellow (or invisible white) cover represents God's Love which goes to all his children alike, but not all his children know what His love is. The first row know and are showing that His love in them is loving each other, and His love is forgiving. The second row is showing that Love is for sharing and for giving to each other. But the third row has not learned all this. Until somebody shows love to them, they may not know what God's love is, and that somebody has to be someone who knows God is in him and them and everything, and that God loves all alike.

(If it were in relief a last row could turn from the light and create a shadow.)

As the golden light of God is on each color of person they become more like God; and althought the Love is there a person

113

who is not loved by a person cannot learn what love is. When he knows God loves him he learns to love himself. And when he loves himself he loves others, and he sees his reflection in them.

Love is for-giving. Love is not for Getting.

The more we love and forgive each other, the closer we feel to God.

"BE YE A MISFIT"

St. Paul said it and he knew from personal experience. I'm glad he said "do not conform to the world, but be ye transformed by the renewing of the mind." So women live longer than men because they can change their mind? You cannot think creatively if you cannot change, and the body too must be constantly renewed.

The world demands conformity, creation demands change, and everybody is a misfit looking for the place where they really fit. The creativeness in you keeps outgrowing places and things, so the movements of people like the movements of the planets are constant, and if they didn't move they would disintegrate and die.

Original people are the creators of the new ideas or fads and thousands of restless people follow like dumb sheep who would rather die with their leader than declare their own originality. In their effort to be an individual and a rebel they end up by their originality being lost in the herd again.

It takes true "genius" to be a genius, because he is the most mist-fitted of all.

He is not welcomed in the average classroom, or always appreciated in the home. Later the world may be wealthier because of him, as it is because of Edison, Tesla, and Marconi. They were banished from the classroom and the greatness they achieved came from within, self-taught.

All great people are self-taught, though they may go through all the proper channels of education. You can take a rose and cultivate it properly, but it will remain a rose. Man makes his own environment; when he realizes this he is not a victim of circumstances, but a creator. "Circumstance was the mirror that revealed him to himself." "Men do not attract what they want, but what they are." "Man is manacled only by himself." "Men are anxious to improve circumstances, but are unwilling to improve themselves. They therefore remain bound." (From *As a Man Thinketh,* by James Allen.)

A teacher should be as a gardener that with love and understanding brings out the best within each pupil. Understand them, help motivate them and let them know where knowledge of the past is found. When they have need of it they will find it. Many dates and names connected with battles of the past are a bore. I know more of the history of England from a humorous book called *1066 and All That* than I learned from all my history lessons on England. Only two dates are given in it. It's a very good book to read out loud for English history class in connection with the other type.

Emphasis should be on developing the vision to see beyond the now, to develop mental control over the emotions, to learn how to get along with others, and to assume responsibility. They should learn to use the mind to probe into the world of ideas that includes those beyond the five senses, and also to be able to analyze what the five senses tell them. There is a book, *How to Survive in the Woods,* which has a world of useful facts that, the world being in its present state, should be known by all. It is written by Bradford Angier, Collier Books, New York, N.Y. With this knowledge you would be able to select and catch or find food and water and protect yourself. Sometimes I ask my pupils simple "survival" questions such as "if no water could be pumped into your home and you have not kept a few bottles handy, where would you get it?" Most are not aware that their hot-water heater would have thirty or more gallons of pure water. There should be a spigot at the bottom of the tank. To get water in remote places a sheet of plastic laid on the ground in slight tent fashion would make the dampness of the ground condense on the under side of the plastic and run into a container for drinking. Or put one or two drops of tincture of iodine in a quart of creek water and let it stand for thirty minutes to kill all bacteria and make it safe to drink. Let some water spill over the top edge of the jar after mixing, to purify the edge over which the water will have to pour.

The children of this age have not gone through a "Depression" which trained us to make do with very little. If our telephones and push buttons and electricity were removed we would really know how misfitted we are to cope with stark reality.

Children should be allowed to collect "junk" (I call them "treasures") and put things together in unusual ways even if they goof. Edison goofed 999 times before he made a good light bulb.

Children's time is too organized. Mothers may want their children's time filled so they will know where they are and think thus to keep them out of mischief. But a child is headed for trouble if he doesn't know how to enjoy himself alone and does not exercise his creative mind constructively. A child should be allowed to play alone with "stuff." (If he is very young, put one of those one-way peep holes in his door.) This is the time they grow from within.

It isn't easy to know whether your son who sits staring into space is plotting devilment or redesigning a carburetor for a car to get greater efficiency, but I do know that you get what you expect out of your children. If you say you trust them and act as if you don't, you've spoiled the whole thing. Appreciate the goodness of your child and you won't have to bear the "badness."

I wish that parents knew they have the most perfect chaperone in the world and it's a free One. If you *know* that

God is everywhere present you will know He is in your child
and in you and the space all around both of you. If you *know*
that God wants the best for all, then ask and *know* that He is
with your child wherever he is and that He, within that child, is
protecting him. This knowing can be used for anybody or
anything, of any age. Only doubt or disbelief kills its
effectiveness. Read Isa. 43:1-3, Deut, 31:6, Joshua 1:9, Deut.
20:3,4, Jer. 32:27. Paul said "The Christ you have to deal with
is not a weak person outside you, but a tremendous Power
inside you." 2 Cor. 13:3, Phillips translation. You do not have
to be a church member to believe every promise in the Book is
yours, but if you believe them you may want to be in a church.
Man needs to belong to a group somewhere.

If you have a creative person in your home he will be a
dreamer who must be allowed to put some of his dreams in real
forms. If it is a "treehouse," don't get him a "treehouse kit to
put up in four hours." Let him find stuff (you don't mind
helping to haul it, but don't be tempted to draw his plans). It's
not the results he needs but the experience. Let him have
animals. He doesn't get allergies from things but from his
emotions, his frustrations, his hurts. Let him be himself at
home, or later you won't know where he is or what he is. Let
them talk to you *without* you giving advice. Is it possible?

If a brother or sister is a show-off, a "genius" may appear
dumb. One way to be an "introverted show-off" is to be
delinquent or sick or accident prone. It's a different way to get
consideration and affection. It would have been cheaper to have
listened and shown affection earlier.

Boys and men are many times afraid to demonstrate
affection to the feminine part of their household. They are
afraid they'll be effeminate. It seems that the true masculine
men don't have this reticence. Men should know that when the
Adam man was complete within himself he was terribly lonely,
so God took most of the femininity and made a helpmate that
appeared truly feminine but had enough of him that she could

understand men. God also left enough of the feminine characteristics in "Adam" so he could understand women. The feminine is emotional tenderness, understanding, softness, permissiveness and the reflective "moon." The masculine is aggressiveness, hardness, rationality, and the energizing, brilliant sun. So a man who does not know the meaning of tenderness will *never* know women at all and if he does not express it he will never have a woman be his "slave" willingly as many do. Those who show tenderness and understanding to each other know that life is worth living even in the presence of any hardship.

Since we're all "misfits" trying to fit somewhere snugly, it would be a good idea for each member of the household to study the others' natures. They are really as different as the animals of the zoo. It might give a clue if you'd ask each what animal they'd like to be and why. It could be that your household is made up of a mouse, a lion, a rabbit, a dog, a cat, and a monkey. Each would have to give up a few of its "faults" to live together.

One way to get an insight into the differences in human beings is to read a really good book on the characteristics of each birthday sign. A good one is Linda Goodman's "Sun Signs," a delightful analysis of all ages.

In the first chapter of Genesis it seems that God made the solar system before he made man, and He said they were for signs and seasons. Now any sign that's put up is supposed to be read, especially on the highway of life.

For instance: There are three earth signs, Taurus, Virgo, and Capricorn, and they are as different from fire as real fire is from real earth. The fire signs are Aries, Leo, Sagittarius. The water signs are Cancer, Scorpio, and Pisces. The air signs are Gemini, Libra, and Aquarius.

These four elements make up our world also and as you study their characteristics you'll get a clue to how water and earth or water and air, etc., are compatible with one another. It is necessary for us to have some of each to be complete and we may be lacking in some of them, so to be complete we must have other people. Can you pin down air? It gets stale if it stays in one place too long. Can fire do without air? Too much makes hot air. Can water and air do without some warmth? Can water be contained without earth to lap against or run between its banks? Read pages 16-19 for more comparisons of these elements. I have noticed that these elements, which also are a part of your environment, as house and yard, will tend to reflect the emotions of the household. Do you get angry with a "fire sign" person and burn something? Note what "element" is your problem and change the emotion to change the problem. Sounds silly but it works. Perhaps an air person needs more fire to inflate herself, and if you don't do it she blows herself up in temper. At the same time you may have air and heat problems in the house, or air in the plumbing, or low air pressure in the water tank. Are you having air and water relationships not in balance? In the paper today was an account of the plumbing in the house "talking" all the time.

Everything reacts on everything, so it is good to have quiet moments at odd times during the day so your world can balance itself before the next plunge. You might say, "Slow me up. Lord," or "This too will pass," or "I'm forever undisturbed."

A young woman friend of mine has five children under six and she said it wasn't easy for her to say and believe "I am forever undisturbed." And especially hard when the baby in a high chair has turned over his milk, another with drippy sandwich in one hand is pulling the venetian blind up and down, and the phone and doorbell ring, but she said, "I said it out loud with conviction, the children got quiet, I attended to the phone and door, and everything was wonderful. You know I'm a Leo and I dramatize everything to the hilt, but when my husband came in that week end, he thought I was sick. I didn't greet him with all the calamities of the week as usual, but I told him I knew how to cope with them." The new drama was heavenly. The first time she lay down for a quiet time, her four-year-old tiptoed in and said, "Mummy, you sick?" and she answered "No, Dear," and the little one left saying, "Don't worry, Mummy, God will take care of you."

Constantly bless the things around you. Would you believe the appliances of your house work better with appreciation? Scientists have researched this and say that plants respond to love, and in my case dying trees return to life, washers and furnaces can rest and go on efficiently, and water pipes mend leaks. We can forget people who help us, so it's doubly hard to remember to be mentally appreciative of the stove and the sink and the refrigerator.

Look at everything as a blessing and it will bless you. That is a law of the universe. Bless every bit of money you spend or give and "see" it blessing those whose hands it touches, and money "planted" thus will come back to you multiplied. This also is a universal law and God's promise.

A child very early begins to see that the earth is loaded with misfits that should fit somewhere. He may start with that little plank with different size and shape holes and he takes from a box blocks and a hammer and learns by trial and error where each fits. Later he may note that a blockhead and a square are perfect under certain needs. So misfits are really perfect when they find their place and it shouldn't take so many years. For 10,000 years we have been told to "know thyself" but as soon as we think we do we find another undiscovered facet and the search continues. The reason we are different and so unique is because our purpose is different. We find it more easily and quicker without that "If I were you I would do thus and so." Nobody can ever be another and if you *had* been me you would have done exactly as I did. Criticism and condemnation, I think, is the greatest sin of all. We note that Jesus did not condemn Judas or even the woman the mob wanted to stone for her sins. A person knows full well the mistake that has been made but when criticized you spend hours trying to vindicate yourself to another. You could have spent that time improving yourself. If another does not criticize you, you work overtime to prove worthy of that understanding. If one is praised for what he does right, there will be fewer and fewer mistakes made.

Up to now we are talking of misfits in abilities and personalities in the so-called normal body where we have no physical reason for not doing all things. This is a much harder condition than one who has a physical handicap. I know that if you are physically handicapped you will disagree with me. May I give you a way to look at it? If I have no hand or arm I am not expected to use it and there are many who are happy to "lend me a hand" because they need to be needed. But if I cannot mentally use a hand which is perfectly good and normal they may think me dumb and stupid, and if they think it I feel so.

Not only do other people desire to help those who need help, but the rest of the body becomes greater and stronger to compensate for the absence of one of its members. This absence makes a vortex, or funnel, through which good comes to the rest of the body. So a missing part or a weaker part becomes the "star" and is given a greater honor than the rest of the body. Read what St. Paul said about it in I Cor 12:12-29. May I give you a few examples? There are great artists who have only one arm, or are paralyzed from the waist down, or have to hold the brush in their teeth or toes, and greater honor is given them because they overcame the body to become great. They are individualized. A boy was born without arms and legs and became a great scientist. Arms and legs can be "borrowed," they can be "hired and fired" but all that he needed, he had. Life rushed to see that he was educated and every bodily need was taken care of.

A farm boy of the 19th century was content with the chores of the farm. His arms were torn off in a grinding machine. Life saw that he was educated and he became a college president.

There is no circumstance that one gets into that God cannot turn it into a good thing. It's hard to see it sometimes but it does no good to mourn for that which it is too late to change.

Some may take a negative approach to the loss of a member and the rest of the body is not allowed to be itself. It feels insulted to have all these good parts wasted just because one "went away." Cannot you imagine the body crying, "So! One member of our group is gone, but the rest of us are strong enough to carry the full load. Einstein said a genius uses only five per cent of his capabilities, so what is gone was not an absolute necessity — the heart of the matter, the desires, the emotions, this is what life runs on, anyway. You cannot compress a balloon in one part without making another part greater. Please, you've got your head and the head is the boss, command us to do your bidding, we'll show you. Don't let our missing member destroy the purpose of the rest of us."

When one part is missing the ESP works better, your radar stays in tune, your "third eye" knows things your two eyes would never have seen, your spiritual ears hear things the physical ear never heard. If we *knew* only the things the five senses know we would be dumb indeed. Your body knows what you tell it with your mind, but if you let another person hypnotize you, you are not your own boss temporarily and your body knows what the hypnotist tells you you know. For instance, he can tell you he is touching your arm with a red-hot poker, instead he touches it with an ice cube. You don't believe what you see but what he said, and your arm will blister where it is touched. He can tell you that you can't lift a small tray off the table — you try and you can't. He could tell you you couldn't talk or see or smell or hear and you couldn't. Now when this act is over he is supposed to erase from your subconscious these lies he has told you and return your body to its rightful owner, which is you. But if he didn't erase it you would remain with these lies which would now be true for you because you accept them as true. That is why it is dangerous for you to let another have control over your mind and body. Only if the hypnotist is good and pure and knows the rules, and it is necessary experience should it be done.

But — we do it to ourselves all the time. It is self-hypnosis and it is wonderful but it can be self-destructive according to the way you use it. You are what you tell yourself you are and what you really believe.

Make a list of what you really wish you were and want to be.

Now make a list of what you really think you are now.

Can you be the person of both of these lists? Do you realize you *are* what you thought you were *because* you believed it?

I can hear you sputter, "But — but — but —." So while you're at it butt over that stone wall you built with can'ts. Soften it up with cans and cans of cans. Get Claude Bristol's book *The Magic of Believing* (Prentice-Hall Pub.) and read about a child that was born to a poor mining couple in a most remote section of the United States. She was full of fancy ideas and imagination and loved poetry and nature's animals and was so different in her nature from all her people that she fancied herself to be a child left with these people at birth, but that she really was the child of the prince of India. She lived and acted as if she were of "royal birth." So convincing was she that when she was grown our President, Teddy Roosevelt, gave her a visa to go to India to find her parents. When Bristol wrote the book she was living in the royal palace of India and was accepted as a person of royal blood. Self-hypnosis, of course. All this was accomplished through her belief backed by action.

"Whatsoever a man thinketh so is he." Your total body members, nervous system, etc., are your servants and must do what you desire if you want it enough to train them. If one servant quits the others move to fill the need. Read often the little book *As a Man Thinketh,* by James Allen. You can get an inexpensive paperback edition from DeVorss & Co.

Now, will you please watch what you are saying to yourself so that you are what you desire to be. YOU ARE WHAT YOU THINK YOU ARE IF YOU THINK IT OR SAY IT DAY AFTER DAY AFTER DAY.

The spirit and soul of you is the real you. Imagine the body after these have departed — it is inert material without knowledge or energy or personality. So that which is the real you is the un-see-able you that was using the see-able you to run around in. Now, this spirit and soul in the body are linked with universal energy, universal love, power, light, and you can have and use all of this that you tell yourself you can have. I'm saying this to try to convince you that if you are not what you desire yourself to be it is because you've hypnotized yourself into believing otherwise and thus your body is obligated to obey you. Now that you know, praise every part of your body into being its perfect self. Give thanks for being able to receive......... (whatever you want to receive). And "what you believe you will receive, you will receive." This was the promise, so be careful that those things bring no harm or hurt to another because everything makes its complete circle and returns to you multiplied. What we all should ask is that we receive that which is for our good and our abundance. The Father within knows what we have need of and our spiritual growth depends on us wanting and accepting what is good for us.

If you are doing what you came to do you will have peace within. There are no big or little purposes, all are of equal importance. The smallest part of your watch is as important as the hand that tells the time. A mother who loves and holds the family together is fulfilling a need a billion dollars cannot buy. If you think you are ignorant you are needed too, as the world would have no need of teachers but for you and others like you. The restaurant owners are happy that many people don't like to cook. You cannot have a single infirmity or quirk of personality that you do not make another wiser and greater because of it, so stay the way you are as long as you can stand it, and when you can't be that way any more, change. For everyone who needs there is one who needs you. Love is forgiving. Love is not forgetting, so when you receive from another anything you must share it by being or by giving. You cannot receive more light without being a greater light to others.

Every part of the body is a symbol of your world of experience or your world of thought. The condition of your body reveals the hope or despair of the thoughts.

Lucille Ball at 17 wanted to be a great dancer. She is a Leo and they (Leos) seek the grand life in the limelight. Her home life was broken, she lived with an aunt and the chances of her being a dancer were slim. So the part of her body that wanted to dance got sick. They called it rheumatoid arthritis of the legs and she lay on her bed for three years. Her legs acted as if she had said, "You'll never make it as a dancer — you'll have to give it up." Now when people are sick many others want to help and encourage them — why don't they do it earlier!! So I can imagine they told her not to give up — she'd be a dancer, they would help her get her training, etc. After being in bed three years she began to walk again and in six years was a famous dancer. The weak part had "bossed the show" and through its weakness brought honor to the whole body.

Too bad the average well child gets so little attention. If you have a child who is giving you no trouble and is well give him attention and admiration so he won't need to get sick or be a problem to be noticed. In the beginning this is not hypochondria but life because love and life are one. "Love or perish." They have found that lack of growth in a person can be lack of love aand appreciation and that children who are stunted are stunted for lack of appreciation or being wanted. This could start at conception.

Joan Crawford wanted to dance also. A foot ailment threatened to stop her before she started but she wouldn't let it and danced to stardom. See the symbol of foot and dancing?

Eve Arden, "Miss Brooks" of TV fame, was so shy about talking that in high school she got sick when she had to recite in class. She has no trouble talking now.

Ray Bolger, the dancer, was a real wallflower, it is said.

In 384 B.C. a boy named Demosthenes was a stutterer. He would go down to the seashore and talk above the roar of the waves, then put pebbles in his mouth to make it even more difficult to talk. This went on for months and years. Is it amazing that he became a great orator? (The Encyclopedia Britannica devoted five whole pages to his life and works.) It might be he became wise when as a youth he was thinking instead of talking publicly. Orators are listened to because they have something to say.

June Allison, actress, with fractured skull and injured back was relegated to invalidism. Six years later she walked and became a swimming champion.

Lee Marvin, actor, had his sciatic nerve severed in World War II by a sniper's bullet. You wouldn't know it now.

When one comes to the point where they see their desired life might be ended they have a choice — to lose the life or to find it, so they choose life and then they have to lose the life of invalidism to find the active life they wanted.

Glenn Clark had heart trouble and arranged his life to cater to it. He was asked to lead a big conference at a high mountain retreat and high altitude is not compatible with a weak heart. He wanted very much to go and told the Lord that since he was called there to do His work he knew He would take care of his heart. And so He did and his heart was OK from that moment on.

A little girl wore braces on her legs for 15 years so she could walk on her weak rickety legs. Awake and in her dreams she dreamed of running, running, running. Is it any wonder she became a champion runner? YOU WILL BECOME WHAT YOU THINK ABOUT DAY AFTER DAY AFTER DAY.

Glenn Cunningham was eleven when he was so badly burned

that "they" said he'd never walk again. This was not his idea of living so he went ahead and became "The Champion Runner." Many years after when a doctor examined his feet he told Glenn he didn't have a metatarsal arch and thus he should have not been able to stand, walk or balance himself, and never could he have run. Glenn grinned sheepishly and said, "Gosh, I'm glad I didn't know that." Glenn and his wife have helped hundreds of young people by taking them into their home with their own children.

Examples of weaknesses propelled to greatness:

Boy lost arms, became great educator. Legs burned so badly was told could never walk, became high jumper. Wore braces for weak legs till age 15, became famous runner. T.B. and pneumonia, became writer of religious books and publisher. Migraine headaches, became world's leader. Ear trouble, good listener as a psychiatrist. Throat troubles, singers, speakers. . . Each had wrapped in sensitivity the symbolic counterpart of his future talent and greatness.

The modern science of acoustics was begun in 1700 by Sauveur, a French physicist, who was deaf and dumb.

For the last twenty years of his life, Renoir painted with his hands crippled. His brushes were attached to his forearms. His work was as good as that done earlier with full use of his hands.

Beethoven, when deaf, transformed the sounds of music he could hear only in his soul to music of the spirit.

Weakness is stronger than strength because it attracts all strength. Watch a two-year-old child on a city street. Even strong people, strangers to the child, rush to protect it. A weakness is a need and need calls on universal energy. No one, even God, can force you to accept what God has for you. You are a son, not a slave, and thus you are free. But even human sons are so stubborn they'll starve rather than ask a loving father for help if they feel guilty. But this Father loves you. He does not condemn you, and when you ask Him and believe it He gives you all He has over and over again.

He says command me — prove —. Now, if you are commanding you must know the nature of what you are commanding. God is Love, Light, Wisdom, Energy, and all things made are His. So you cannot command Him to give you other than what He is and has.

But if you receive what He has given you and you use it to create ungodly situations, you are "sowing the wind" and will "reap a whirlwind." And still he will keep giving you the "wind" that you may through experience learn how to use it. Read the Prodigal Son story. Poverty is a state of ignorance about supply. Wealth can be another type of ignorance about supply. The middle class may be the wisest because they know supply is daily and comes daily and is gone daily. This is the manna that His children received and could not hoard.

For myself, I ask that He give me what is best for me for my learning, and best for me of the abundance He has. Then I won't be saddled with things I don't really want or things that create extra problems. He is Love, and Love-is-for-giving-not-for-getting. If you want some "hating" done, or "getting even" He cannot help because divine love does not know what hate is (read I Cor. 13). Yet God is within you and does not leave you though you go into a den of vice. He says "I'm there with you," not as a condemner but as a loving Father.

We don't really like this idea. We'd rather He'd be "up there" and we'd rather think that we can hide our thoughts and actions from Him. We wouldn't want even our best friend to know our every thought, because best friends would offer advice or criticize. God doesn't. Love does not criticize or condemn, but when you know He loves you in spite of yourself you will make amends to the error.

If only children had always known that God is pure love — that God is All there is, that being All and in all He is in each of us for "instant" advice and comfort and need. We came from Him. In our own consciousness we pretend we go away from Him and return to Him, but if He is All then there is no other place to go. Since we live in a world that our own thoughts and imaginings make, we live in a heaven or a hell or in between, and in the space of a minute you can "be" in either state of mind, heaven or hell.

Our life consists in doing, being, succeeding, or making mistakes and correcting the mistakes – other names for sowing and reaping. And until you understand you cannot sow and not reap, and cannot reap what has not been sown by you in thought or deed, you will believe life is unjust.

This is an orderly universe and everything was made Good.

Our will to be free and make our own mistakes and not check with "the blueprint" before we go ahead is really not BAD at all. Most of man's own creativeness has come from fixing what he has broken because he wouldn't listen to that "father within." This has created employment in all the repair shops such as hospitals and rehabilitation centers for people's bodies and all other fixing places for "things" bodies. These interesting fixing places make people more prone to be careless with themselves because we have insurance for repairs and we don't want to waste anything.

The clothes designers and manufacturers cover mistakes in thought and diet as well as reveal what was well done.

The preoccupation with "this body" and what it wants probably occupies 98 per cent of Man's time as well as his thoughts. Seems a shame since you can't take it or its earthly necessities with you.

So this earth is the kindergarten of all our solar system as well as the universe and we know that until in this flesh we could see only Good we will continue stumbling and blundering back to our Good. Because we are a part of Him He knows all about it, and feels our hurts when we make our mistakes but He is a good Father. He can't do for us what He can't do through us.

A friend once said, "I get so tired of people in the church

urging me to do so many things for God. I need to do things for myself."

I thought of it and realized that God doesn't *need* for us to do anything for Him at all. He IS and has everything. All He needs us for is because He has everything to give and He made us in His image of love and light that He might give us love and energy and light. As many as receive He gives extra that those who will not see Him in the abstract will see Him in people. As they receive love and light from people they become receptive to Him, the source of all love and light and energy.

Love is for giving — love is not for getting.

More than getting love, we must have someone to love. A woman in her maturity who lives alone says, "I have a lovely home, I'm a good housekeeper and cook, but I don't have a man to share it with, no one to do things for, no man to love." God gives with no thought of return but desires that His children will give His love and light to others and they to another that all may be filled with light. You cannot really give anything away because as you empty yourself God is filling you with better of everything.

To achieve true oneness with God is true fitness and any seeming misfitness in the world doesn't matter any more.

"Have you ever realized the most incredible fact that your bodies are integral parts of Christ Himself?" — I Cor. 6:15.

The world has been wonderfully blessed by the misfits, the physically handicapped, the 4-F's, the sick and the too old. In the last 10,000 years there have been only 365 days (not years) when some country was not at war with another. Misfits have good minds, even great genius, and they did not have bodies fit for fighting wars so they as scientists, writers, teachers, philosophers, artists, poets, inventors, have helped hold the world together. Many soldiers come back also handicapped. Our studies in rehabilitation will help ease their way also.

Prenatal Influences

The only time a mother is in complete charge of the nature of her child is the approximately nine months before birth, so take advantage of this. Here are some examples:

Mother had to spend much time in the hospital during pregnancy. The girl child became a doctor.

A woman desiring to become a doctor had to give up plans when she became pregnant. The boy child became a doctor.

Pregnant mother engaged in water sports till late in the pregnancy. Child "took to water" with no fear.

Colored mother and father with little "beauty" of face wanted a beautiful baby. They surrounded themselves with beautiful baby pictures and mother was so happy she sang hymns during the months of waiting. The child *was* beautiful and became an opera singer.

Dr. Clymer, M.D., did research during a fifty-year medical practice. In a book called "How to Have a Perfect Baby" he gave accounts of the parents directing the nature and interest of the child-to-be. It is the easiest way because it doesn't take long after birth before the child is "directing" the parents.

In another account of Dr. Clymer, an uneducated couple wanted their children to be professional people. The parents, for the first child, studied in their simple way building plans and drew house plans and the boy became an architect. With the other two they "chose" other professions, "and the children became what their parents thought about."

If you have already been talked about out of this idea, I *dare* you to experiment. The Bible Tells of Hagar and her child, Samuel and his mother, Moses and his mother, Mary and her son, Anna and hers. All planned for a purpose.

"Thought in the mind hath made us. What we are by thought was wrought and built." — James Allen.

Stuttering

A stutterer is likely to be a brilliant and deep thinker and thoughts run through his mind faster than the words can be formed. He "holds" your attention to him by stuttering. (Those who have nothing to say talk real well.) Listen to him as if you had plenty of time and don't insist on him telling his thoughts till he's ready. Then no criticism or too much advice or calling attention to how he says it.

If God is All and in All, can there be anything which is not holy? Everything has a time, a season, and a purpose and we take His holy things and create that which is out of time and purpose.

Since God is unchanging is He not as powerful to work "miracles" today as when He did them through Jesus the Christ? The difference is that Jesus was a clear believing channel. "If thou canst believe all things are possible."

THOUGHTS AND WORDS CAN KILL

In Mark 11:12 and 20-28, remember, Jesus cursed the fig tree for not having figs on it, even though it was not the season for bearing.

What was the lesson He was teaching? To punish a dog for not climbing trees? Is this story in keeping with Jesus' nature? The next day they passed by the fig tree and it was dead. Peter said, "Look, Teacher, the tree you cursed has died," and he answered them: "Remember this: If you have faith in God, you can say to this hill, Get up and throw yourself in the sea, *if you do not doubt* it will be done for you. So when you pray believe you have received it, and everything will be given you. *And when you stand praying forgive whatever you have against anyone so your father in heaven can forgive your sins.*"

"Life and death are in the power of the tongue." – Prov. 18:21.

"You hold in your hands the very word of life." – Phil. 2:16.

Did you know that every destructive thought you have that could be symbolized by a gun, a dagger, a knife, a spear, a sticking pen, can be "picked up" by the mind of those who are not well controlled? They find it easier to act out the same idea with the weapon they have in hand.

134

Communicate

Every gentle loving suggestion plants a seed that comes up at the right time and flourishes. Every angry command flings a seed that may get results immediately but it is sick and tries to die as soon as possible.

Nothing is more important than talking with your child when he or she wants to talk and has something to say.

If one cannot communicate with loved ones and you can't take it any longer, you unconsciously choose a more attention getting way. It's called accidents, sickness, sulking, temper. At first a whisper, a whimper, but when it becomes a scream it's difficult to cope with. But it's still saying, "Love me, I'm important. I can't talk to you, you don't want to understand. I can't go on this way. My own world has not cared while I lived – perhaps it will take notice how I leave it."

*

Is the thought behind your wishes (prayers) "I don't care how much it costs," or "If it is good or right for me at this time." Your every deep persistent desire is answered on the material level or on the spiritual level.

*

Dr. Alfred Price is rector of St. Steven's Episcopal Church in Philadelphia, head of the Order of St. Luke, an international, interdenominational organization for spiritual healing.

In a conference at the Edgar Cayce Foundation (A.R.E.) at Virginia Beach, Va., he gave these views, "That prayer must be made for the whole man, not for a particular condition. Prayer must not demand healing. The patient and others for him must surrender to God, God's love; must yield to truth, not facts. God does not answer your prayer but your belief.

"Our prayer for another must be that God works through us as He wills, not to answer your wish. Jesus never used 'Thy will be done' in cases of healing. In Gethsemane that prayer was one of commitment, not resignation. 'Thy will be done' in healing is right only if we believe that God's will is good will."

Do not say "if it be Thy will," but "Thy will is good." "If it be Thy will" is an escape clause. Doubt destroys prayer.

Healing is forgiveness, of self and others; relaxation; partnership with God.

Life is a Jigsaw Puzzle

Select a beautiful picture that would be symbolical of the life you lead or would like to live. It may be of a quiet country scene or a busy city or perhaps of a circus. You would see colors in each from the darkest to the lightest. There are things hard and soft, sharp edges, and places that flow into each other.

Mentally see this picture cut into the number of days of your life and you will lift one piece at a time from your "box" and live it. Today is it a black one? I hear you say "This is going to be a bad day; I feel it coming on." If you remembered the picture, it was the shadow on the patio where the tea table was waiting for your friends. But no, you have decreed, and you proceed to produce the pageant from your dramatic mind. First the dishwasher floods the floor and you go into your act and only the baby and the dog and cat are your audience. Instead of quietly putting papers on the floor after pulling the plug you scream, and your screams frighten the "audience", the cat and dog start a fight. You put them out. The baby "upchucks." More screaming, but now there are two of you doing it.

In the midst of all this the neighbor runs in bringing your dog who, in his fear of the home situation, has blindly run into the street and been hit. The neighbor stays with the child while you rush the dog to the vet. The car *tries* not to start so you'll calm down before driving, but you force it and dent a fender in your confusion.

"Now whatever caused all this?" your husband asks that evening. What you will say will make a long story, but the truth is you started it with the THOUGHT of expectation of a dark day.

Next time you pull out a dark piece, clean out the closets, or do the dirty work you have put off too long, and you'll end the day feeling like a saint rather than a martyr.

Many of your children's illnesses and accidents begin or occur on the days you are terribly concerned over what you think is an important episode. The "neglected" child is unconsciously trying to let you know people are more important than things.

In the movies we may see husband and wife separated, too proud to admit each is sorry. The child gets sick, hurt or lost and the parents are brought together by a common sorrow or fear. Don't tell me children don't know more psychology than parents.

Did this beautiful picture have to be put together with such dramatic disasters? If that is your desire, the answer is yes, but *you make your day* and your lessons are harder than was ever intended on the divine blueprint.

*

Hay Fever Vaccine?

Bees take pollen and make honey. Pollen causes many people to have hay fever. Many hay fever sufferers have cured themselves of hay fever by eating the honey and chewing honeycomb. Predigested pollen "fights fire with fire."

I AM A LOVING CUP

We sing, "Thou art the potter, I am the clay. Mold me — fill me." He's trying but I am so "resist-able."

Our body is a container made from the elements of the earth as a vessel for Him to fill of all that He is. To fill, not for us to use for ourselves at once but to be given to others that He may through our lifetime keep giving to us and through us.

Why shouldn't we keep it? What He gives us is "unseeable" and we get the "seeable" things we need by giving it away. Haven't you heard that the only things you really have are those you've given away? In God's Kingdom things don't make much sense unless you use His intelligence to see it. Suppose you have an idea for an invention. A friend of mine thirty-five years ago said to a party of friends, "This radio is so hard to tune with all those buttons. Why doesn't someone find a way to push one button and have it affect all the others?" She was an artist and would not have been able to tinker with the idea herself so she gave back into the "ethers," the airways, a good idea, and in a few years her radio could do just what she had asked. The idea, the need, is flung into the "mind of God" which fills all space and the answer which was in the same mind rushes to meet it. You know a few of them, the safety pin, the sewing machine, radio, TV. etc. All were made of the spirit of God in man connecting with the basic materials his WORD has made. This was stirred in the clay pot of man's mind with the need of the world, and out came the "whatever."

So if a person receives God's Love and Wisdom and Intelligence and Energy and keeps it for himself alone, it gets stale and stinking because God never can give him fresh love and wisdom. These people think they *have it*! They know everything! Why should they give of their knowledge and supply? They might run low sometime, and they are too proud to ask even God, so they hoard all their good. This is what is known as living death, or "Dead 1956, Buried 1982" could be put on their tombstone.

So we who know God and believe His promises and what He is, find that we can't give anything away that we do not receive more of what was better for us. And the greatest gift is Love. God is Love and is always giving. God keeps nothing for Himself because He IS. I cannot do or give anything to Him. I do not give my spark of light back to Him to show I love Him; I give it to another who is in darkness that they will know His light, and immediately I have more light than I had before. I give my love to another that they will know what God is and Love pours into my "bowl" from all the world.

What shape and capacity is your bowl? It does not matter. It only matters that you be what you are, but the best of what you are. Tiny teaspoons go to more fancy parties but the cups and pots and pans are the most needed in the working world. If you're a teaspoon, others are teacups, some are the teapot type, and others are the pot you boil the water in. We still need the one who is the long pipe that brings the water to the kitchen, and the end of it you can turn on and off, and this is good. So what a party of containers! And what fun because each gives a different kind of joy and humor and knowledge which, when mixed in this big pot, each has the knowledge and love of all the others.

Those of us who know God's love and supply must teach those who think it is their "lot" to be poor. In 2 Cor. 9:9 we are told, "he gives generously to the poor, his kindness lasts forever." Generously means more than you need. In 2 Cor. 9:10-11 Paul said, "And God, who supplies seed for the sower and bread to eat, will also supply you with all the seed you need *and* make it grow, to produce a rich harvest from your generosity. He will always make you rich enough to be generous at all times, so that many will thank God for your gifts through us."

What more do you expect? All He asks is that you believe He loves you, believe He gives you what is best for you, and that you share with others, that they too may believe and receive.

For Love is for giving. Love is not for getting.

If you would hear God speaking to you, He would be saying, "I love you – you are my very special child. There is nothing you can do that would stop my love from coming to you. You are a part of my perfect body and every part is made to express itself for the good of the whole body. When you will not let me give my love and qualities to you, you block me. If you who might be a part of the vital artery to my hand feel that you are unworthy to be it, you block me and the block you put in my bloodstream blocks the line to the hand and fingers and they can't do their work. All because you couldn't believe that God who is All would not be aware of 'poor little you' and your needs.

"Have you not heard 'for want of a nail in the shoe of the horse the battle was lost'? Your earth is a battleground only because many men couldn't believe that I, your God, would keep supplying them with every good thing. They thought they had to take from others and then put what they stole behind barricades. The earth is mine and everything in it is mine and all people are mine and I would have given them all knowledge of Supply and they would never have wanted for anything. Oh, well – I still love every one of them but they won't believe it. It makes them feel guilty when they think of me and they try to believe I do not exist. When they are no longer in a body and they can then see the truth that *I am Love,* they wish to return to those on earth and tell them. But all of my angels and my children who know cannot get through to them as long as their minds are closed. It's easier to teach those who have 'come over the threshold' because most of them have called me with their last breath and as I have promised, I have answered."

Sometimes a person disbelieves because he has had such a hard life and he cannot see why he deserved it. The sowing and reaping is sometimes so far apart that we find it easy to believe that we get many things we do not deserve. We are dependent on so many people and things and man-made laws and governments that if any one of them fails us actually or in our minds our security is threatened. Yet everything is cause and effect. America is still reaping the sowing of the Indian wars when we took their land, and they in turn were reaping at that time their own harvest. We do not know their time of sowing or what it was.

Much of our reaping in "seeable" things are the crops of our thoughts which were — we thought — a secret that only I, you, knew. But every thought is creative and goes forth and returns to its creator. "Be not deceived, God is not mocked; for whatsoever a man sows that shall he also reap." Gal. 6:7.

Do not be hurt if you do a favor or kindness out of your love of God and it seems not appreciated on this earth. What you do in earth for which you are paid and are told you are appreciated, you have your reward for, and if it were on a ledger of outgo and income it would be marked off and the book or page sealed. But what you do for Him that is not appreciated or noted on earth is marked on the pages "in Heaven," and your reward is constantly multiplying and doubling and redoubling and the invisible loving cup of you in God's sight spills over and showers the earth with blessings and we call them falling stars or, sometimes, shooting stars.

How's Your Perspective?

Perspective is one of the things we learn about in painting pictures. When two or more things that are alike are placed in a picture, the smaller one is drawn the more distant it is. Sidney J. Harris pointed out in his column some time ago that the mind reserves this law, and that this illusion is created by desire. What we have on hand, our own, seems small, and what we crave from afar or what another has seems more desirable and larger.

It's the same old grass being greener on yonder hill. Or, "I wish my wife was as good a cook as yours." "Your husband is so sociable and gracious and understanding."

"One swallow does not make a spring."

Don't Be Just a "Do-Gooder"

When your heart, Christ in you, "tells" you to do something, you will be doing it in love and you give your love with it. That person feels the love and it is a warm feeling forever even though the gift was really very little. But if you give because you should and your purpose is a "gold star" somewhere, it does more harm than good. If you give a coat and food and give not love, it may keep the skin warm and the stomach full — but the chill in the heart is not removed. If you had not given it then another who does have love of them will see their need and love *and* supply will be met. Do not give a gift to compensate for the bitterness between you and another, for every time the object is seen the bitter memory is recalled. Before the gift, give love.

When you give to an organization to be regiven and you will never see the people, send love to them in every object. When you pay your bills or give money send blessings to those whose hands it passes through and those who receive it. Whatever you bless will be a blessing to you, and whatever you give in love comes back tenfold. This is one of God's wonderful laws when used rightly but it comes back to you with the "curse" *if* that is the way you send it out.

We are constantly giving of our time and life for another — but if it's done in love, our life force is generously renewed. That is why those whose "time" is filled can always find "time" to help you. God is timeless.

God Loves the Dead End Kids

Have you reached that end of a blind alley and there is no other way to turn and you give up? Then ask God for the answer. He could have told you earlier but you weren't asking or listening. You are the only gift He wants. When your will is His will, miracles happen. "If two of you (your Christ self *and* your human self) will agree on any one thing, it shall be done."

Is Your TV a Friend?

If your T.V. is a necessary part of your waking life, don't let it "hit" you while you're down and asleep. You couldn't find a more worldwide innocent brainwashing machine. While you are conscious your wisdom can "talk back" to the silly ideas and plots, but while your subconscious is in charge, and it's like a primitive child, it takes everything as the "gospel" truth and acts upon it — makes its own show to fit the words with *you* as the principal character. You are told that you have tired blood, are the next heart attack victim, one of your family will have cancer, you're irregular, have tension. "I'll kill you!" Do people shun you? There are cases of heart attacks that occurred in sleep while they were told they would be the next victims.

If a mustard seed can grow a huge tree or move a mountain — then our T.V.'s are going to hatch some mighty airborne birds and vultures. (From Prevention Magazine, Feb. '68. — Rodale Press, Emmaus, Pa. 18049.)

Radiation from TV can change physical and mental growth of infants, especially before birth, and affect the general health of children and adults. This warning from biologist John Nash Ott on light radiation. He was awarded an honorary doctor of science degree from Loyola University of Chicago. He insists that no one should sit less than fifteen feet from front, further from sides and backs of color sets, which have much more voltage. Radiation goes through walls (lead sheet can stop it). TV's in hospitals are dangerous. Children become tired, unambitious, have glandular changes. The Underwriters Laboratories' inspection does not include tests for radiation. Normal average set on two hours has radiation of average X-ray exposure. Sets were recalled in 1967 that were sending out same as eight X-ray exposures per hour. Dr. Eugene J. Sternglass of the Westinghouse research laboratory warns of even as much radiation as one X-ray exposure in the early development of the embryo (1952). Radiologist Edward E. Sheldon of New York told a House subcommittee in October, 1967, of the hazards of TV. *But — we must protect our industries. A lead shield in the TV would make the TV set cost a hundred or so more. And we are allowed to remain bombarded with radiation and thus become less mentally alert.*

A Charlotte, N.C. newspaper (May 9, 1968) wrote that the same opinion and proof was given by Dr. Ott, head of the Environmental Health and Light Research Institute, at the North Carolina Medical Society meeting. Fatigue, nervousness, overstimulation, damage to mental and physical health of the family, are associated with those who watched TV for thirty or forty hours per week. He blamed the X-rays.

One of the past great radiologists said that even the radium on the dial of wrist watches was harmful. Therefore it is advised to remove watches at night. Many people sleep with their hand near their head. I note that the clock radios have very large dials and a radium area more than twelve times the area on wrist watches. The top of the head is one of the most sensitive sections of the body. It contains the pineal and pituitary glands, two of the most spiritually important of the seven centers of the body.

*

The Bible shines Light on all your problems and pulls you back into balance. For some it says "become as a little child, bear one another's burdens, cast your burdens on the Lord, love one another." To others it says "put away childish things, bear your own burdens, love yourself that you can love others, receive light that others will see your light."

If you prefer an "outside" God, then verses have pictured it out. But if you desire to believe He dwells within you, you will find those verses also. Is there any spot where He is not?

*

No matter what pickle you get yourself into God likes "pickles" and if their hearts are right He can turn them into dill-ies of successes.

*

"We are but broken lights of Thee; Thou, O Lord, are more than we."

COLOR IS NATURE'S HEALING FORCE

Take the cut glass prism from your chandelier and hang it in your sunny window. Let the Sun of God come through it and throw those seven healing colors into the dark recesses of your room and mind, and watch yourself come alive as you catch your breath with the vibration in the colors. Put colored glass bottles or objects in your windows and feel it recharging your body's "batteries." Eat the foods that have imprisoned the healing colors from the sun; their color "healing" properties are the same as for the color in glass or fabrics of nature.

It is said that each of the ductless glands is "fed" by a different color. You have heard that "we are what our glands have made us." We have been told the glands are the storehouse of past memories. If we can feed them and "balance" our memories, we should give some attention to them.

These are the colors for the ductless glands:

Adrenals: bright purplish-red. Pineal: blue-lavender. Pituitary: blue, yellow. Thymus: gold-pink. Thyroid: gold-green. If your doctor says you're "flagging" in one, use color too. The Solar Plexus, the emotional brain, needs the entire rainbow of colors, and the prism in the sun is an exciting way to provide them.

It has been proved that acne on the face can be cured if you sleep on a cloth or pillow of fuchsia (a cerise-red) for 14 to 21 days.

146

To cure bed-wetting, use on bed amethyst (towards the violet-pink) and pajamas of that color. Also say silently to the sleeping child, "When you have the urge, you will rise and go to the bathroom." "If thou canst believe, all things are possible."

As a rule, the normal craving you have for a food or color shows your need for it. It will usually irritate you if you don't need it. Learn to use your inner light for guidance.

People who are sad and do not love themselves may need loving friends and gentle colors to bring them out of that mood and nature can provide the colors.

"And the leaves of the tree (of Life) are for the healing of the nations." – Rev. 20.

Nature pulls us out of the winter with the yellow leaves and bright yellow flowers. This is the color to restore nerves, to purify and cleanse the body. The body is recharged and as the sap rises in us we want to spring-clean and tidy the earth and uncover sleeping beauty. Some of you may remember the sulphur tonic in the spring.

Yellow, the brightest color, really does make us brighter, and slow children are helped mentally by yellow color, worn or looked at, or eaten. Students, wear yellow to your next exam.

The next abundant color nature gives us is green, the most healing color of all. Made from the yellow rays of the Sun and the blue of the sky, it is literally heaven brought onto our earth plane for the healing of the nations.

So eat lots of greens, too. You may call it rabbit food but Dr. Aurella Potter, endocrinologist, recommended rabbit food for executives. He said, "Middle-aged rabbits don't have a paunch, do have their own teeth, and haven't lost their romantic appeal."

We have about four months to store up the health-giving greenery, so bask in it, walk through it, and store green in the body and the memories. It is the cooling color to offset the heat of summer sun. All things come to us in pairs, in opposites, and we use them to balance as we choose, as sun and shade.

At the end of summer we have the cooling months just as the leaves, in a burst of the warm gold, yellow, orange, and red colors are storing the heat of summer to nourish nature through the cold winter months.

We use these bright colors in fabrics and flowers through the drab months to balance and cheer.

Music, too, has the power to heal, to stir, to agitate, and to disturb. It would be wise to give some study to the "things" in our environment that could be made more harmonious — sounds and colors. We are all different in our needs; meat to one may be poison to another.

Blue is also healing and so is purple — both are spiritual colors. The deep cobalt blue is very cooling and soothes inflammatory conditions of mind and body. It constricts, shrinks, eliminates, slows up conditions of body and mind. Blue is a very slow vibration.

That reminds me — I was a blue-eyed, straight-haired youngster, and was dressed in light blue most of the time. I was timid, shrinking and slow. The word most said (and it was needed) was "Hurry." It must have made quite an impression on my subconscious because now I can't slow up. Parents, *never* doubt that your child hears you, though it may be 40 years later.

Color is one of the most beautiful of the gifts of the Spirit. Learn to appreciate it. Look at a color in nature as if you have never seen it before, store that memory so you may think it into existence at any time your body needs it. Every part of your body needs different "colors" at different times, to cool, to warm, to energize, or to calm.

Learn nature's wisdom in the use of colors. See how nature gives us bits of the bright reds in the autumn, brief hot sunsets only occasionally. We can go wild in the use of reds and create excessive energy, nervousness, even riots.

I wish the designers of schools, who may need red personally, would not have the doors painted red or orange. It accelerates the children's energy and rebellion against school as they enter. It is not encouraging mental work but a "call to arms." Why not paint the doors yellow or blue or green?

Same idea when decorating your child's room. If the colors are so exciting the child can't sleep (colors vibrate in the dark) then change them, or put a blue glass over the night light and use blue or green pajamas and bed clothing. And if your little rebel loves red and you have red bedspreads, take them entirely out of the room for the night.

Red is tiring to the eyes and yet the car designers have a row of red lights on the back of many cars. This inflames the eyes and mind of whoever drives behind them. When will they learn that accidents are mostly psychological, not mechanical?

You can get "Color Healing," which is the compiled works by 21 leading exponents of the uses of color, from Health Research, Mokelumne Hill, Calif. 95245.

Get a Rainbow

You can buy yourself a rainbow. Go to some of the bargain department stores and ask for a "cake saver" made of clear plastic called "Festival Ware." The plate part has a fluted edge and when hung or set in a sunny window, three prismatic rainbows spread across your walls or sink or counter. It thrills you so much you get your chores done while the Light of the Sun comes through.

*

"Everyone who feeds the lusts and passions or yields to the lower nature crucifies the Christ within himself, plants fear in the subconscious mind, so that the things he does bring his reward according to the thought seeds he has sown." – Alice Bailey.

Pink Is For Boys, Blue For Girls

Somewhere somebody "goofed". They didn't know the effect of color on people and things and thus we have created a generation of young people that it's hard to tell which are girls and which are boys.

This was my conclusion when I read of some scientific discoveries about color. They tested the effects of color on flowers which were male and female. When the pink light was directed on them for a length of time, the male flowers flourished and became healthier and the female wasted away. Then they put the blue light on the male and female flowers and the male got weaker and the female flowers got healthier.

Do you see what we did? At the most impressionable time of the babies' lives we used the color that suppressed their maleness and femaleness. We stifled it with ribbons, and painted walls and furniture and toys of the wrong color for that sex.

Everything happens for the best.

Perhaps this togetherness will stop wars, domestic and foreign. And didn't Jesus say, "We are all one"? And Paul said, "We're all one body." And in the almanac the one universal man has every type of person a part of that One.

A by-product of these findings on color we can still use to shape our bodies. Since pink makes maleness more male and slender it can be worn to reduce you, men or women. It makes you so alert that the increased activity of the body helps to reduce you. And blues and greens make you increase in weight, more feminine, that is, curves. It tones you down and relaxes you, which is an aid to gaining. So wear your cool colors to your outside activities rather than discard those dresses, and slip into a hot pink house dress and get to work. Later, pink nighties and pajamas are an idea, too.

When I published my pink book I started wearing pink suits and dresses to match and I went down from 110 to 90 before I read about this. Now I'm wearing blues and greens before I disappear.

Plants *Do* Love and Suffer

St. Francis knew it, now scientists prove it.

Plants and trees, shrimp and beans, have emotions. Cleve Backster of Backster Research Foundation in New York City proves it. He attached electrodes to the leaves of a plant to measure the rate water rises in a plant and found added information. A leaf was dunked in hot coffee and showed no emotional stress. This proves (to me) that vegetations "know" they exist for mankind's nourishment and they live to feed the lower animals also.

Everything lives for something higher in consciousness.

Then he decided to burn the leaf and at the moment of his thought the P.G.R. tracing indicated emotional stress as if in a human. This happened also to the leaf when live shrimp was dropped in boiling water and Backster wonders if living cells signal death to other living cells. Frogs stop their "singing" at a given split second. This doesn't always happen to people in church.

This experiment explains the success of the "Green Thumb" people. The thumb is *will* power, remember, and people who love growing things bend their will to the nature of growing things — they *are* gardeners, not dictators.

The person who wrote this information for the paper suggested that if ones neighbor grew better strawberries, he could send threatening thoughts to them and stunt them. I wish he had known that *every* thought, good or bad, comes back as an experience to the sender, and since plants and animals are tuned to the mind and spirit of God more than people are, the strawberries would have known it was an idle threat.

WATCH YOUR WORDS AND THOUGHTS

Creation, and destruction, began with a word, and still does. The word became flesh, and still does. Your affairs and your body show whether you have used words constructively or otherwise.

"Physician heal thyself," and "To thine own self be true." If you say you love God and do not love his child; you, me, the truth is not in you.

Are you loving his precious temple, your body? Every part, every tiny cell has labored every second since your beginning. Yet, you seldom speak to it except in a critical way. If you treated your friends or acquaintances the same way they would have left you. Some of your body "friends" may have left you already, they just cut out and disappeared and other untrained "friends" had to do their work. Some of these, feeling unappreciated, are unhappy and are thinking of quitting. If these faithful, marvelous body parts had been your part time servants, you would have praised the work of their hands, heart and mind and seen that they were comfortable and happy. Instead, with your body always listening, you have said they were weak, feeble, bad, ignorant, ugly, and at times lumped them all together with "they're just no good at all." You have even paralyzed one of the members when you're in a paralyzing situation and blamed them.

Now, it's time for a housecleaning. Start seeing all the good that is there. Through reading my book I hope you know the duties of each part, and what it thinks about life so — stop frustrating it with procrastination and indiscretion. Tell your body it does not have to act out physically what you're thinking because you will solve it mentally. Read again "How to diagnose your Ailments." Learn to be truthful to yourself and others. You are not *supposed* to do everything you're asked. — You do not *need* to be a perfectionist in every department of your life. You cannot be everywhere at once. Be kind to your friends.

Now I would like to tell you another way to quickly know "Who's the Matter with You," so you can love them and forgive yourself. I have resisted putting this in this book for many years because it will hurt some peoples' feelings (so do operations), but sickness costs are going up and these truths do not show up in tests or X-rays. A paralyzed woman found by reading my book that her inability to move was because her husband hadn't sent 3 months' alimony checks, and it cleared up immediately. It would be wonderful and quicker if forces of people would show in those X-ray pictures. Most of the time you'd see that the problem wasn't that important, but your body thought you wanted to "really show them" how hurt you were. Every cell in your body is only a few months old and acts young. Let it do it rightly.

This is your kit for quicker knowledge. Get a farmers' almanac that pictures the Universal Man body with all the different birthdays having charge of perfecting some part of the body. Until some liberated woman got in the press room and switch the plates, all ancient almanacs had the right side female with water and earth signs (read pages 16-18, 21, 22).

Now — remember that St. Paul and the Bible kept saying we are all one body and if any part suffers all suffer; and that every planet had a different quality. That if you have anything against anyone forgive, agree with your opposite quickly or you are the loser. That each has a different talent or gift. The least thing can get the greatest attention (sand in your sandal, for instance). Until you are perfect you cannot *see* God.

All these ancient truths were first put simply in the farmers almanac in A.D. 9, but the masses have only used it to plant their crops and only a few saw the universal oneness of all life. The trinity of the 4 elements joined as one makes the 12 pointed star. Each starts life at some point and begins the return to the Father in the center of their being. Each person travels a different road to perfection.

Now with this almanac picture in your mind list the birthday signs of the people in your life that matter to you negatively or positively. These are those who are now or who have leaned on you. Some are those who's manner of parting still "bugs" you.

Resentments can kill slowly. Bring into your conscious mind your memory of those who long ago have hurt your feelings and forgive them, even if its not possible to get their birthdays.

These buried hurts are the causes of the sicknesses of the soul and body. Get rid of these and I'll tell you how not to let it happen again.

The people in our lives are constantly calling on us for help and understanding but they sometimes don't want to bother us, so, as a child touches his mother to get her attention, they will touch us emotionally on the part of the body that is their Ego Sun sign; as for a Pisces on the foot, Aquarius on the ankle, Aries on the head, etc. The nature of their dilemma could be the nature of your sensation: paralysis, cramps, burn, cold, stiffness, a twitch, etc.

As you are deciding *who* they are start directing love and understanding to them. As you continue with your work, visualize the stress leaving them and being flung into God's great incinerator, the Sun, the consuming flame. Now picture the energy from the Sun sending life and light to the earth, flowing through you to this needy one and others. Thus you and they also are renewed. Now your body sensation has gone. If not, the message may be your own body talking to you of its needs. Attend to that for yourself.

Many people have responded in a negative way and thought this pain, this stiffness, was the beginning of a major ailment and by giving it thought created one.

I know many people whose body problems were of the part the "Almanac Man" had given to some loved ones. Those people had called and reached out to them for love and understanding with a desire to patch personality conflicts but there was no response, no truce or peace and the war was accepted in the physical body. Try to attend to these problems mentally quickly. To hurt another is to hurt ourselves, because all are one.

Study the places of your present and past ailments. Some people don't like themselves and hurt themselves in their own Sign's parts. We are our own worst enemy. Forgive yourself and others and remove stress daily as I have told you how to do. Those forgiven people will feel the load lifted immediately and your body will feel lighter and younger. Love everybody and release them to their own divine plan. Criticism has always lost us our Eden.

*

Sylvia said, "You may not be able to keep a bird from lighting in your hair, but you don't have to let it build a nest there."

YOU BECOME A CREATIVE PAINTER

It is said that to express all sides of your creativeness you must write a book, have a baby, paint a picture and build a house. If you have never painted a picture let me help you get started. From the day you paint your first picture, nature will never before have been so beautiful.

Because I am basically lazy and the "work" I do is to hide that fact, I love to evolve quick and simple ways to do things that "smart" people take a long time to do.

If you were in my studio and wanted to paint landscapes and would become as a child — relaxed, expectant, willing to make even a mess and enjoy it — I could have you painting as would an artist in an hour. For a little while, you must forget to be a perfectionist and you find a release in expressing yourself without fear of criticism.

Paint for your own joy, not to impress someone else or to get *a* picture for *that* blank place on *that* wall. You can do that later, but forget it now. And if you're one of those sensitive creators that's afraid of being laughed at, cash in on that fear — *be* a clown. Our brainy philosophers never make the money the comedians do.

A perfectionist acquaintance visited my studio one day. I don't remember that she ooh'd and aah'd at my work, though they usually do as they are expected to. But, she did say, "I can see that you'll never need a psychiatrist." I laughed and

156

answered, "If I ever did I'm sure he'd have to see *his* psychiatrist." Many times later I've thought of what she said. I wonder what she *really* meant?

Now, for the first time I'll try to teach by remote control and try to get you to create enough mess-ter-pieces so that some will be masterpieces.

Don't ask your friends what *they* think of them — do you ask people what they think of your child and their advice on "bringing him up"?

This painting, this clay modeling is a "fun" thing, to take you out of yourself so you can come back and be your best self. If you have children, it is amazing how you rise in their estimation if you have painted a picture — it takes you out of that "servant" class that *they* have put you in. They will *see you* with new eyes, too.

Subconscious Painting on Paper

INSTANT PAINTINGS BY THE SUBCONSCIOUS

Let your subconscious paint your pictures for you; it already knows how. All you have to do is have the materials and put them at the proper places for action. All your life you have filed away those beautiful pictures your eyes beheld. You have said thousands of times, "If I could paint I would love to have a picture of that." *Now you can.* They will come tumbling out and you will find they have hatched others you do not recognize. This Space Age is the instant age so here goes.

Take a flat smooth or interestingly rough board and put one or more colors on it, not too thick, not too thin. Have wetness on the whole board and be quick, before it dries, to put a piece of white paper on the paint and rub "its" back. This is when the real you gets impressed.

This is the process of the nine Ps — Plastic (board), Paint, Paper, Press, Pray, Perceive; then say "Phew" or "Pretty" and then be sure to Procrastinate a long time before you say it has no merit. Sometimes it takes twenty-five years before one can see merit even in a child.

Make at least two dozen the first time you do them. If you get one real good one you can consider yourself equal to professionals; their percent is one out of fifty according to the famous watercolorist Eliot O'Hara with whom I studied many times. Even Babe Ruth is known for his hits, not his misses. Creative work by any artist is like the iceberg. Three-fourths of it he keeps out of view.

Subconscious Painting *"My Island Hideaway"*

Later, at your leisure, sit and "take a trip" through each painting, viewing it from all sides. Find the trees, the animals, the people, the flora and fauna of nature. Some of my good ones took me from weeks to a year to see the potentials. Pretend you're a landscape architect viewing the land and note what minor changes could bring out its beauty. Don't rush to do too much and destroy its natural beauty, but cooperate with what is already there. You can enhance it with watercolors, watercolors in small felt tip pens, and oil pastelles.

Once you try the simple way above described, you may want more control. Suppose you *want* to do a landscape. Put the sky color at the top, overlap it with middle distance far away trees, and the simple foreground colors. NO DEFINITE THINGS can be put in the picture now successfully. Wait and brush them in later while wet *after* you find what you pull up. They must be pulled up from the "top of the sky" or the accidental trees will be standing upside down. A road is easily made by swishing the edge of a dry sponge on the painted board where you want the road to be. Repeat the color of sky on the ground and it may look like a lake. If you want the wind to blow in your picture, pull from near one upper corner. When you get a too wet Foggy picture drop it lightly back on the board and pull up *without* rubbing.

You know, of course, that we attract that which we love, fear, or think about constantly. There were interesting examples in my classes. A five year old put shades of green on her board and when she pulled up the paper she had a perfectly formed whole bodied Peter Pan sitting on a rock in the woods. An eleven year old girl during February "Lincoln week" got a perfect profile portrait of Lincoln *but* she had put half the board green and the other half purple.

The picture illustrated, called "My Island Hideaway," is in a brownish yellow color. I later made the definite trees with a brown small felt marker. The slab of white which is now the roof of a house was changed at the right side to conform with

Subconscious Painting *"The Leprechauns"*

the slant of the other side. Horizontal streaks with oil pastelles were made on what I wanted to look like water.

"The Leprechauns" picture is in soft blues and blue greens. The tree was put in several weeks later but I didn't sit and travel through the picture and see who was already living there. So I almost knocked off the nose of a perfect Leprechaun. You see him with his nose facing the tree above the left side limb. He wears a pointed hat and so does his little brother on the other side of the tree. Notice the cape over the larger Leprechaun's shoulders and the lion cub's face embroidered on his chest. He must be the "King, the Lion Hearted" of the clan. Naturally, you see the owl, the unicorn, a devi head in the fork of the tree, and the many animals and lakes below.

The other "subconscious" on paper with a big tree is made in soft greens and browns up into an amber yellow sky. Do you see a shaggy mountain goat perched on the rock at the left?

*

You can do Isometric Painting. It is mental; not physical. Just lie back in your chair and pretend you're painting a picture of something you are looking at. Note the light and dark areas, the colors. Cut a rectangle in a black piece of paper or use the little black "frame" of Polaroid Film pack when it is discarded. Hold it near or far from your eyes and "frame" what you're looking at. When you've done this many times you'll just have to use paint or chalk and really do it.

See list of materials on page 188

*

If I'm very early how do I know whether I'm the bird or the worm?

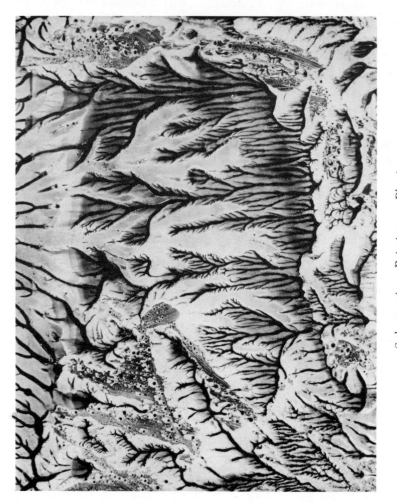

Subconscious Painting on Plastic

SUBCONSCIOUS PAINTINGS ON PLASTIC

Take a sheet of milky-white thin plexiglass and quickly brush on it a color or colors of medium consistency. (Watercolor, showcard, tempera, poster paint, or dry color mixed with water.) Press another piece of plastic on this and pull up. Hold up to let light come through to reveal what you have. If you don't like it, press it again. As you see in my examples, there are always trees or bushes. You will also see eyes peering out at you and you will see animals and people in some.

In the one with two trees, "Winter's Lake," I had pressed paper on the plastic instead of another piece of plastic, and didn't get the many tree formations. In the three-tree picture three of the trees were too large to be at the top of the snow banks almost half way up. So I trailed the trunks to the bottom with a brush and later created a tree bark effect with a magic marker. Then on the back of the picture and above the snowbanks I put yellow Flomaster ink and it looks like trees and snow at sunset. In the other one I did not do *any* extra work on it. It was painted by "slopping" yellow and black on the piece of plastic and then pressing another piece on it.

Sometimes you want a print of what you have, rather than leave it on plastic. Press paper on it and pull up from "top of trees" section. Now look at the plastic held to a light and you'll

165

Subconscious Painting on Rigid Plastic

see that it's even more beautiful. (A light near the floor will let you see the effect without the wet paint running down.)

When you get one you want to keep, let it dry and spray with acrylic or plastic spray once or twice; it becomes permanent until you use acrylic remover to reclaim your plastic.

Experiment by sometimes rotating the top plastic on the bottom one and pull up at an angle. It can look like "Creation in the Beginning." Do not wash off colors after each picture, but add others to it. The grayed effects you get will be lovely. Don't work too slowly or be too careful where you put colors, or some will be too dry before you print it. I don't like to make rules, because the best pictures can be made by breaking all the rules, but I don't want you to be disappointed because you "left the flour out of your first biscuits." If I were demonstrating it to you, only a few of mine would be good. The difference between an amateur and a professional is that the professional has done thousands more pictures and shows his best; like an iceberg, two-thirds of his work is hidden from the viewer.

Doing "subconscious" paintings is a wonderful way of relaxing tension and "stilling your mind" to "take you out of this world." When you "return," you are as refreshed as if you've had a vacation. Never discard any of them, but sit while you rest your body and go through them for possibilities. Sometimes a two by three inch section is a *gem* and can be framed with a wide mat for emphasis. The blue ones make beautiful Christmas cards. On Christmas I put a coat of white glue (like Elmer's) on a small white board and, without waiting for the glue to dry, dribbled blue Flomaster ink with a few squirts of lighter fluid and left it to dry. Several weeks later I saw what I had — a seated mother and child with Joseph standing at the right, staff resting on the ground. An angel with wings was on the left and a cathedral window was in the background. To make it more seeable to others, I highlighted the tops of shoulders and head, and put haloes on mother and child. At Easter time I had made a dozen large ones and decided to give up, as none seemed to be good. I was using oil and turpentine and printing them on coated fingerprint paper. I saw there was much oil left on the glass slab, so I flowed turpentine over it to soften and clean it but, instead, took another piece of paper and printed it. There was "the stone the builder rejected," early dawn with the glow of sunrise at upper right. Three women with shawls over their heads were coming to the Tomb. Many symbolical figures and animals were in the gray woods at the left, but the most important was the standing mother and child.

One other Easter there appeared Christ in Gethsemane, with the three prophets in the background.

You will attract to you that which you are, even for the moment.

To put this to the test, once, when I was making a picture, I thought of a past situation which had been very distressing to me. I pulled these past resentments up and replayed the record as I pressed the paper. I was not surprised when there appeared a perfect portrait of Dante's Devil. I hope I got him out of me.

*

"And Out of Yourself, Create. . ."

"Look for your own. Do not do what someone else could do as well as you. Do not say, do not write what someone else could say, could write as well as you. Care for nothing in yourself but what you feel exists nowhere else — and out of yourself create, impatiently or patiently . . .the most irreplaceable of beings."

— Andre Gide

FLOMASTER INK ON RIGID PLASTIC

Upon moving into a house with the old plastic tiles falling off the wall behind the shower, I solved the problem by getting rigid clear plexiglass to surround the tub. I dribbled an undersea scene on it. When finished I used gesso in a cream color to paint over it and had it installed with the picture on the back of the plexiglass away from water and steam. After ten years' use there has been no water erosion. Go get clear or milky-white or colors of scrap plexiglass from companies that make the plastic outdoor signs.

You may put thick or watered down white glue on it before dribbling inks. Tilt it or blow it or drop lighter fluid on it to get exotic forms. You may, even after it's dry, put drops of the glue anywhere on it and in a few days it will be a "jewel" of the color on which it was dropped.

Experiment: You can draw a design on paper on one side of the plastic. Put design under the light plastic and you can see the design through it. Mix black Flomaster ink in a squeeze bottle of white glue such as Elmer's. Squeeze on the plastic along lines of the design. Let it dry. Now you can squirt Flomaster ink in the sections with occasionally a bit of lighter fluid with a medicine dropper for better control. This will look like a leaded stained glass window.

Idea: Take several milky plastic pieces and on each put different combinations of colors, warm yellow, orange, red on

Flomaster Ink on Rigid Plastic

one and cool blue, green and warm and cool combinations on others. Read up on color healing book listed under "Color is Nature's Healing Force." Lend or give these to your sick-a-bed friends according to whether they need pepping up or cooling off. Deep cobalt blue for high blood pressure types who should shun large areas of reds and red orange in their homes or offices.

Spray these with acrylic spray and let air a few days before taking to a sick room.

Dye your own glass with Flomaster ink. (Directions under "Materials for Creativeness.") This dyed glass from broken rear window of a car, can be used to make the Christmas or year-round cathedral candle holder. Put this dyed glass between the outside footed goblet and the smaller inside "juice" glass that contains the short candle. The light flickers through the many colors. This also could bring "Light" to a sick person.

Creative Thinking Is Wealth

Longfellow could take a worthless sheet of paper, write a poem on it and make it worth $60,000.00. That is talent.

Rockefeller could sign his name to a worthless piece of paper and make it worth millions. That is capital.

Uncle Sam can take an ounce of gold and stamp an eagle on it, and make it worth $20.00. That is money.

A craftsman can take material worth $5.00 and make it into an article worth $5000.00. That is skill.

But God can take a worthless, sinful life, wash it, cleanse it, and make it a blessing to humanity. That is Salvation.

Where is God?

I sought my soul, but my soul I could not see.
I sought my God, but my God eluded me.
I sought my brother, and I found all three.

Sculptures by the Author

FIRST, BE A "MUD DAUBER"

You will surely be as good with your first clay modeling as I am a writer, in trying to write "how to do" in words, when I've always demonstrated with my hands and very few words. I've re-written it nine times and I almost gave up. So, if clay figures are something you want to do, I will again try to make it simple enough for you to start.

Get familiar with your clay; take a handfull and squeeze it; make shapes like ◿ △ ▭ ○ ⬯ ⬭ or ▭ . Pretend these are gift-wrapped objects and try to imagine what is in them. Then, with your "X-ray vision" and your fingers, trace out on the clay what it is. Add several different-shaped lumps together, or make a horse head out of different size triangles.

Each piece must be knitted together eventually or, in drying, it falls apart, but now it's more important that you get

173

your creativeness to sprout and enjoy it than to preserve the evidence. (As a walk through the woods does you good, even if you didn't take pictures of it.)

Also, I've found that many experiences in life you would not choose if you knew all the details of them before-hand.

This is to be a fun thing for grown ups. Just use the same "know how" that you've always used in the kitchen and get familiar with clay as a new medium. Clay is a combination of earth, water and air. As you model, it must have little air and be pliable. Later all the water escapes as it air-dries and, when *absolutely* dry, it can be kiln fired at 1500 plus degrees and made as hard and permanent as stone. So, it must be kept wet while working by putting thin plastic over it; press out all the air pockets and tie it so no air will get in. Thus you can work on it for months. If left for any length of time, put a wet sponge inside the plastic with the clay.

If you want to make a head, use about twenty pounds of ready-mixed potter's clay from a pottery or art shop. (about $2.00) Get a wood block or board and a one-half inch plumber's flange and one-half inch pipe to screw into it, and attach it to the center of the board. If the hardware store has only six-inch lengths of pipe, get two and a connection, or put a dowel stick in one of the six-inch to make it long enough. Slide the block of clay down over the pipe and you are ready to begin.

Hands are the best tools of all but, as you work, you'll need shapes your hands don't have, so collect a big nail or pencil or inkless ball-point pen, a springless clothes-pin, manicure "aid" from the top of some nail polish bottles, an orange stick, and a hair pin wired to a pencil. You'll feel like a "pioneer" and realize the genius was in you, not "store-bought" tools.

After working in secret you'll have something your friends and even relatives will exclaim over and they will rush out and buy you some "How to do it" sculpture books and some professional tools. I once did a bas-relief of a movie star for a

T.V. show and my tools weren't large enough to show, so I got a large can of sardines and used the "key" opener for my modeling tool. To start shaping the head, make it look like an egg in an egg cup. Remove clay from where you don't want it to where you do. Be a little bulldozer. Cut out clay from under chin to make an egg head. If you make a little girl with hair to shoulders, you don't have to have a pipe in it to keep her from losing her head.

But, if *on* a pipe it must be pulled off before it dries more than a few days and let a little hole at the top of the head connect with the hole left by the pipe to help air dry from the center, also. A non-shrinking pipe in clay that shrinks one-twelfth of an inch can break the clay. Big heads must be dried slowly for weeks.

Place your fingers on each side of the head and thumbs half-way down where the eyes should be; dig out or press up clay to forehead; put on some clay for the nose, letting the two thumbs slide down each side. Put a little "mountain" of clay under nose, unless you prefer a toothless-hag look.

Place the two thumbs in center under nose where mouth should be and fan out and down. Roll a bit of clay, if you don't have enough to push up, and put straight across at bottom of upper lip. Let sides blend into the cheek and chin. See, it looks like a covered pie in a pie plate! You may have to add more clay for a chin, or have an "Andy Gump" chinless face. Let the eyes look asleep at first, showing the roundness of eyeball within the lid. Now observe people's eyes. You've already found you had never really been conscious of how a face is put together.

I hope you have an old "lazy susan" and have your clay head on it and have turned it often to see if it looks human from *all* sides. If it looks too old, you need more head above the eyes — add some.

You may now see that you have George Washington (he has been so imprinted in our child's mind, he comes out in every sculptor's work) in the beginning or, you may have an old witch, or an aborigine, or voodoo doctor. Finish this first one up as "that" and tell your critics that's what you meant to make. *Never* tell someone you are making your husband or child for the first one. You could get so much helpful advice and criticism that you'd give up. Perhaps somebody will let you run your thumbs over their face, to get the feel of a human being.

It's interesting to make red clay hair and lips and eyebrows on a buff clay head. While the head is wet, but finished, take red clay from clay bank, and make liquid clay (dare I suggest a blender), to make it like coffee cream consistency. Strain through a tea strainer to get the sand out and paint the parts needed red. The two clays will dry together. (This is called sgraffito when one color clay is put on bowls and vases over another color and a design scratched through one to the other. Try that sometime.) When this head is absolutely "bone" dry you could spray it several times with mat (dull) finish acrylic spray or clear enamel spray and leave the clay colors as its finish. Everybody will think you very clever.

Heads can be antiqued with shoe polish, painted with interior wall paint the same as your walls. A coat of lacquer can be the undercoat. Experiment on old dry lumps.

If you want your statue to look like metal, as lead, pewter or bronze, go to a hardware store and get a tube of plastic aluminum and some lacquer thinner. Mix some half and half and brush on raw *dry* clay head. Each thirty minutes or so put on another coat until four or five coats have been brushed on. This will look like lead or pewter when aged. To make it bronze greenish or brownish get that color of shoe dye like "Lady Esquire" shoe coloring. Put on with brush and cloth and let dry over night. Take the back of a "silver" spoon and rub the high places on head and hair to bring out the metal look. Don't over-do it. It can fool even the professionals. The beige shoe coloring is interesting also.

This plastic aluminum was made to repair metal but I've used it on badly broken plastic or other materials of statues. Glue back the broken pieces, tie together till set. Paint all exposed areas with the aluminum mix. Take a spatula and put aluminum direct from tube into holes or to build up missing parts. Dip knife in lacquer thinner to smooth and shape. It can be sanded and smoothed with a lacquer thinner brush.

This can be used to make inexpensive statuary look expensive for indoors, or outdoors on clear days.

I forgot to tell you that Flomaster ink can be put on objects made of milk glass and eventually it looks like a rare marble.

Go to the library and get books on clay and sculpturing. There are lovely books on it in the children's department, I hear.

You will also want to try to do a bas-relief (pronounced baa as in sheep).

Put an inch or more of clay in a big "pizza" plate, or bottom of cake saver, a movie film box lid or bottom (if you put thin plastic in tin first, the clay won't rust it) and smooth it out a little bit. Draw a head profile on it, leaving much more room in front than in back of head. If you're right handed do the head facing left, if left handed, the right. Thus you can see what you're doing and you need all the help you can get. Later you'll tackle anything from any angle.

Remove about one-half inch of clay from the background near the face. Let your thumb flow lovingly up and over and in and out on the face as you push clay up to get eye socket and eye brow, bumpy nose and cheek bones. Every curve flows into another curve. Forget your hand and think of the effect you want to get. Again you are a happy little bulldozer pushing clay from here to there. Add a little clay for the area over the ear but from the lowest part to the highest you should try to limit to three-fourths of an inch in depth. It can even be a modeled drawing on clay. See your encyclopedia for ancient sculptures and bas-reliefs.

Long hair on this too will save you doing ears. Do the hair with your fingers and thumb as if you were gently brushing the hair of someone you love. Blond hair should have very little depressions to create dark shadows; brunette, deeper shadows. Don't rake or scratch the hair unless you want to; this is your head, do as you please.

Bas-reliefs, unless in thick clay, will have to be cast in something like plaster. You can get plaster in small quantities at the drug store at ten cents a pound or by the hundred pounds for $2.50 delivered at a builder's supply. No 1 moulding plaster is the finish plaster on plaster walls. Go to the library and get a book on casting in plaster. There is a new product called Hydrostone that builder's supply firms have, a harder and finer quality. A strip of linoleum makes a good ledge to put around a circular model. Rubber or plastic bell cord is a good non-rustable hanger.

And now you *know* more than I knew when I had been studying for five years. Happy years are ahead for you too.

*

To reclaim old dry clay lumps put them in plastic container

and cover with water. Let set for several days or until soft throughout. Pour off clear water on top; within next few days put lots of newspaper down and cover with a tough cloth. Dump the clay on it and let partly dry; turn by lifting edge of cloth. Keep doing this until the clay is in good working condition again. Put in a plastic bag or plastic container with thin plastic pushed against top of the clay to prevent drying. A wet sponge on top of this and a tight lid is a good idea. Old plaster pieces against too wet clay absorbs wetness.

Inherited Ailments?

We love to blame our ailments and our personality quirks on our ancestors. Grandpa's temper, Uncle So-and so's weakness or obesity. How about being yourself and controlling you? But then — don't get so fired up about "being yourself." Who else could you be? Keep improving yourself in body and mind. Your cells are constantly being remade and you're the one that can say "be more perfect or more imperfect." And "as a man thinks he is — he is."

*

If your creative nature seems all dried up does your hair and skin become temporarily dry? Write me your findings on all these ideas in this book. I'd collect statistics, too.

EGG SHELL MOSAICS

These look like fine tile work and make a beautiful hanging picture or will cover boxes and could even be used to make the top of a coffee table if glass is put over the top.

The first time you try this take *dry* brown and white shells and press down on a flat surface spread with white glue (as Elmer's). As you press on the shells they will break into finer pieces and it will look as if you've spent hours fitting the pieces perfectly. You do not have to cover the whole surface but should unless your background is beautiful, as painted gold or silver, etc. You can also cut shapes with scissors *before* the egg white is dry and they hold together.

It takes white glue about two hours to dry and you can look at it occasionally to see if any are trying to "run away" from Elmer's glue.

When dry brush the white glue mixed with a little water over the whole thing. While still wet (or later) squirt Flomaster ink over the shells. You may paint with a brush if preferred.

These are gorgeous and you'll love them. Children from eight to eighty get real excited over them.

> Do not wish to be
> anything
> but what you are,
> and try to
> be that perfectly.
>
> —St. Francis de Sales

THE STAINED GLASS "WINDOW"

To make a stained glass window, buy an old stained glass window from a wrecking company and reclaim the lead. If you can get one with clear colors of glass, do so — most are milky colors: Lead can also be purchased new from a stained glass company. If you can't get that type of lead now, start with squeezing plastic aluminum from its tube to make the tree or design or just an abstract. This is the way I made the picture window in the illustration.

I took a piece of clear plexiglass to make the rigid base of the picture. (Take a one-third inch strip, and with double faced tape, tape on the outer one-third inch of the perfectly cut plastic, or you'll never be able to frame it.) This also keeps the liquid glass (Clear Cast) from running off.

I picked from my pile of old lead a section that looked like it would make into an interesting tree. When I was sure, I cut the top piece, using for limbs the already attached lead which I cut off at a length to look natural. Taking strong scissors, I split the outer ends of limbs in half, a few inches down, then each half into half again less far down and so on, till it had the appearance of a real tree. For the trunk I put two or three strands of hammered-out lead and later put plastic aluminum in the cracks and holes.

When my tree was cut and ready and the plexiglass was clean and dry, I arranged the tree on it in close contact. I mixed the catalyst with Clear Cast and poured it along the tree trunk and limbs and out to the edge, starting at the top until what I

Stained Glass Window

had mixed gave out. Quickly I dropped the red glass beads on the tree limbs for blossoms or leaves and yellow and orange "car glass" for sky. I let them drop and settle as "they" pleased as I found the facets of the glass sparkle better by not being level with the background.

This went on to the "land" area, where I used another string of beads which, to me, now, were cedar trees on the horizon. The different shades of dark green grass with additional pieces of ocean-washed and ground-smooth pieces of green and brown glass for rocks. Later, I took pieces of lead, cut out my name and glued it on.

I mixed some more Clear Cast with the hardener (catalyst) and streamed it over where I felt it was needed. The next day I mixed some more, and with a brush that doesn't shed hair, I brushed another coat over the whole thing.

If it seems not to be drying you can put it in a warmer room, or put a light or heater near by, but if it gets too warm it will buckle.

I know because I've made every mistake.

See "Materials" section for making holes to hang without framing.

One of my pupils took out her swinging bathroom window, put plastic aluminum in a symbolical design, and put on the glass as I described it above. It's beautiful at night to the passers-by and in the daytime to those within.

Another friend took the lead after removing the old glass and shaped it into what appeared a rearing horse and rider and hung it over her fireplace. It was most effective. Clear Cast will have the running speed of cool honey, so prepare to contain it.

If you don't want a rigid plastic sheet or a framed piece of glass to back up your project, then roll out a one-half inch or more of clay on a piece of cloth. Place cloth on top and roll with rolling pin until big enough to lay your lead or iron design. Put thin "Saran" Wrap plastic over the clay and press your design somewhat into the clay. At the outer ledge of the design you may turn up the "Saran" Wrap and push clay against it to "dam" any flow. The "Saran" Wrap pulls off the Clear Cast easily.

I found an old-fashioned fluorescent light diffuser. Three years later (I'm slow) I took out the rigid brace and wired the two ends together, making a metal "rose" window similar to my design on this book cover.

Since this Rose window had twelve equal sections, I put colored glass in each to represent the twelve signs of the constellations and the center as golden-yellow for the Sun.

You could go to an ornamental iron works and get a design in wrought iron and pour Clear Cast and glass in each section. (I try to judge how much glass each section needs.) Put glass in cup with liquid glass and stir it together, then, when I dump it in, every surface of glass is covered and the drippings make the bottom surface.

You could use only Clear Cast mixed with a color and it would look like real glass. If the edges of the design are rounded, be sure the Clear Cast comes up on both sides of the curve to grip it.

There are colored plastic chips which melt at low heat. Someday I will take a wrought iron design and put it in the oven to pre-warm, so it won't buckle and jump in the oven later. Then drop these plastic chips in the sections, piled up to allow for melting and filling air spaces and bake it. First, I'll check to see how high a temperature it needs, or whether it will catch fire, so I will have fire equipment handy (My Aries ascendant is already "fire" and together with my Water Pisces Sun, gets me in hot water, as the fish bites off "experiences" too hot to swallow.)

Plastic smells when cooking. They say that some of these plastic chips can be shaped and cut when warmed. Investigate it. You can get a five pound bag of plastic granules (cooking crystals) from American Handicraft. Spread a layer of aluminum foil on a cookie sheet and make into a simple triangular Christmas tree, with the trunk long enough to stick in a bowl of clay later. Sprinkle small glass chips on the tree, not letting the glass pieces touch each other. Sprinkle more granules over the glass pieces. (The granules melt in the oven and hold the glass, which does not melt.)

Bake in the oven at 375 degrees for ten or twelve minutes. If you forget and it becomes glassy and loses the lovely frosty look, put a few more granules on it and just leave it in the oven another minute.

I put a wire, such as a straightened hair pin, up the trunk, into the main part of the tree within the unbaked plastic, to prevent breaking. But if it breaks, sprinkle new granules on seam and rebake it.

*

Three ways to relieve excess tension:
1. Blow your boiler, take pieces to doctor or dentist or psychiatrist.
2. Lose all friends and acquaintances who bother you.
3. Take rebuffs and problems as valuable lessons you may have needed.
4. Read "be ye a misfit" again page 119.
5. Nobody really enjoys being with a perfect person anyway. It makes them feel inferior.
6. Read the lives of the great. They all have plunged into "the dark night of the soul" and they have come out shining.

ART MATERIALS

Carried by Hobby shops, art supply stores, school supply firms. They have materials, give advice. Order beautiful free catalogue from American Handicraft, Box 791, Fort Worth, Texas.

Watercolor paints used in "subconscious" paintings are sold as tube colors, as Tempera, Showcard and Poster paint, dry powder or already mixed. White glue is water based, known as Elmer's, Polimer, Champ Wood Glue, etc.

Plastic free squeeze bottle at your favorite beauty parlor. Rigid plastic has many trade names; Plexiglass is one. It's clear and all colors and white. Pierce holes in it with red hot ice pick. Saw it with tape over line to be sawed. Call sign companies for scrap.

Liquid plastic is "Clear Cast" at American Handicraft and you make it any color you wish.

Oil Pastelles, small felt tip watercolor pens. Flomaster inks in color in squirt cans. — Same ink is in "Magic" markers.

Paper: white drawing, rice, shelf paper, construction, try all or any.

Plastic aluminum and lacquer thinner from hardware, paint stores, and "Pep Boys."

Plaster: No 1 moulding plaster from builder's supply.

Clay from art stores, pottery, manufacturing.

Clay tools to "make do," big nails, popsickle sticks, spring clothes pins without the springs.

Textile tube 4 feet high makes modeling stand. Lazy Susan for turn table.

Glass: Broken rear windows of cars. Call places that install new windows to save you the old; stained glass window makers. Broken bottles are dangerous to use unless immersed in plastic. Try laying sharp pieces on sheet of rigid plastic, lay other plastic scraps or big sheet over it and bake in your oven. Ask a plastic company if it would be a fire hazard. Hobby houses have boxes of tumbled glass for sale. Wrecking contractors have stained glass windows, etc.

White pipe cleaners are good throw-away brushes. Linoleum strips or semi-rigid plastic is good to put around circular plaque for pouring a plaster cast. Strips of clay rolled and cut can be used if necessary.

Get a jar of Dupont "Pro-Tek" protective hand cream ("The invisible glove") and rubber surgical gloves at drug stores near hospitals.

You don't *need* an easel for anything except oil painting. Turn a kitchen chair over a table and prop drawing board on inside of legs. Makes a perfect easel for drawing, pastelles or oils.

*

Dial *A* For Art Information

Please, except in dire emergency, and unless you have a simple question, do not write for further art instruction. If you do write, enclose a stamped, self-addressed envelope. I am so behind with all my work it might take me a year to answer. I would love to hear of your successes and have pictures of them. It might make an inspirational booklet for others. You grow as you search and you find much more than you were looking for. So knowing too much or having a ready-made kit sometimes spoils the creative germ in you. Don't try to be perfect, just enjoy yourself. The bird sings because he *has* to express himself. Be a bird.

You are as near information as your nearest telephone and shops are waiting to answer your questions and sell you the material.

ZONE THERAPY

The "feet first" picture of your body on the following pages looks like a Humpty-Dumpty person (MS). It is a Zone Therapy Reflex map of the Male and Female body Halves and their pressure points.

This Humpty Dumpty figure mapping man's body's parts of male and female halves is for real. Use its directions to get or stay well.

Feet are put down and cramped most of the time and they say it's difficult to get that blood back up hill through those tiny veins. Without help and exercise its slowed circulation accumulates little crystals, which we call corns and calluses and sores and spurs.

You can read the emotional causes in the chapter on the particular part of the body given on the chart. To massage daily would prevent them getting sore and possibly erase the build up of the emotion. Happy feet are those that bring good tidings.

You can massage them while hands and mind are occupied by taking two prickly hair curlers, put them on a pencil or dowel stick of six to ten inches and put it in an old nylon hose, tie and turn it back over the rollers and tie again. Now while sitting or lying down, massage both feet. Between the toes area and the top of feet can be done with your fingers and knuckles.

The Pituitary, Adrenal glands and liver are the most important. The Pituitary is the leader of all the other glands.

189

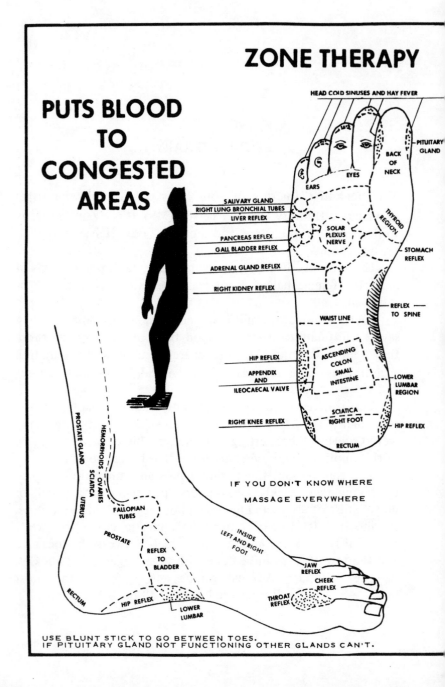

REFLEX AREAS

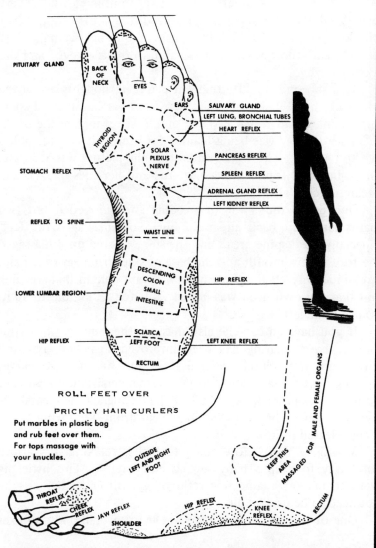

PITUITARY GLAND

BACK OF NECK

EYES

EARS

SALIVARY GLAND

LEFT LUNG, BRONCHIAL TUBES

HEART REFLEX

THYROID REGION

SOLAR PLEXUS NERVE

PANCREAS REFLEX

SPLEEN REFLEX

STOMACH REFLEX

ADRENAL GLAND REFLEX

LEFT KIDNEY REFLEX

REFLEX TO SPINE

WAIST LINE

DESCENDING COLON SMALL INTESTINE

HIP REFLEX

LOWER LUMBAR REGION

SCIATICA

HIP REFLEX

LEFT FOOT

LEFT KNEE REFLEX

RECTUM

ROLL FEET OVER

PRICKLY HAIR CURLERS

Put marbles in plastic bag
and rub feet over them.
For tops massage with
your knuckles.

OUTSIDE LEFT AND RIGHT FOOT

KEEP THIS AREA MASSAGED FOR MALE AND FEMALE ORGANS

THROAT REFLEX

CHEEK REFLEX

JAW REFLEX

SHOULDER

HIP REFLEX

KNEE REFLEX

RECTUM

THE HANDS HAVE THE SAME REFLEXES AS FEET. YOU CAN MASSAGE
THE ELBOW TO PUT CIRCULATION IN KNEE ON SAME SIDE OF BODY.

Examples of money-saving cures. A woman had spent $2,000 trying to find a cure for a paralyzed cheek of four months duration. When she saw the cheek reflex and massaged it, it cleared up in a few days.

Another's infected left eye of five months cleared as she read this book section about the head and massaged her two middle toes on left foot. Six years ago another woman's left second "ear" toe was sticking its nail into the toe "eye" and she asked me why.

This gave me the idea that one can read thoughts out of the zones of the feet also. I asked her if her ear had h-ear-d some unpleasant gossip which her eye should see if it were the truth. (You see the ear was being blamed for hearing it.) So ear pokes eye to check it. The woman admitted the picture was accurate. She called and found it was *not* true and her toes relaxed and became friends again.

One day I did a lot of weeding and enjoyed it but two nights later my back and head hurt, so I massaged the feet, especially the "spine area" and the spine cleared up. I massaged the roof of my mouth and the base of skull from ear to ear and I reminded myself that I really *didn't* want help in that weeding and that my own head was *not* at fault for telling me to do it. So headache left.

If you have an earache also massage the gums back of your molars. Even hearing has been improved this way. Ear and throat are very closely related in action by the two nerves running next to each other. If you have a persistent cough have your ears examined. A man who had coughed six years was found to have a hair growing in the ear drum. Removing it, the cough cleared up.

Massaging feet before going to bed is relaxing. It's also a good way to keep a baby regular and happy. "This little pig went to market" game *was* reflexology. Bitter medicines may not need to be used at all.

One of the best inexpensive books for overall body reflexes

is "do in" (address below). It tells that the outside flesh of the left little finger (as well as the toes) is the beginning of the heart reflex up the arm. If your heart seems too slow or irregular, do a little finger work. From an eye witness account comes this good news. A person may be in a coma after heart failure. If another places their palms against the victim's, their "jumper cabled" hearts will beat through the victim's. Two people on either side of the bed could be like two battery jumper cables. This has been tested on a heart machine.

When one has had an operation, massaging its related zone on the feet would relieve tension and may ward off adhesions.

A woman who was afraid to talk publicly because her jaw locked when she laughed, massaged that sore little toe and her jaw didn't lock any more. (I hope she had something to say.)

You can discharge negative energy and recharge your body by sliding bare feet on a wool rug. Walking on rough ground and sand is good also.

Many feet and bodies are burned by the synthetic clothes and shoes which are made with formaldehyde. It can be worked out of clothes but check these man-made shoe materials and take them back if in two hours your feet are red.

Be kind to your feet and thank them for their good work. Their job in life *is* to be stepped on but they want to be appreciated.

Source of books

"Do in." Happiness Press, 1607 N. Sierra Bonita Ave., Hollywood, Cal. 90046.

"Stories Your Feet Can Tell," by Eunice Ingram Stopfel, P.O. Box 8412, Rochester, NY 14618.

"Zone Therapy" by Wm. H. Fitzgerald M.D., Health Research Mokelumme Hill, Cal. 95245.

CARE AND FEEDING OF ME

By the time you first read my book, some part of your body might have been sick of the way you were impressing it with frustration and then calming it, or feeding it the wrong food. You can have a fine car and a perfect driver but if the timing and mixture of oils and gas and air and water are wrong you have a problem going places.

To understand better the care and feeding of the mechanism of this beautiful temple we live in may I give you help in your research too.

Order from Reader's Digest their series of about 24 reprints: "I am Joe's or Jane's heart, liver, ovaries," etc., and you will be better able to understand you.

"Nutrition and your Mind" by Dr. George Watson. Overcoming anxiety and depression through diet and vitamin-mineral therapy.

"A New Breed of Doctor," Alan H. Nettler M.D. He stopped giving drugs and uses nutritional methods. The book tells laymen how to use it and treat low blood-sugar.

"Food is your Best Medicine," Henry G. Bieler M.D., says: "The cause of disease is not germs, the use of drugs for patients is harmful. Disease can be cured by proper use of proper foods."

"Diet and Health" compiled from Edgar Cayce readings. Quote: "We are physically and mentally what we eat and what we think."

194

"Eat Right and Keep Fit," and other paperbacks by Adelle Davis.

"Food Facts and Fallacies," Fredericks and Cailey.

"Know your Nutrition" (and others) by Linda Clark.

"Mega-Vitamin Therapy," Adams and Murray. They quote that "low blood sugar is at the root of drug addiction, hyperactive children and disturbed personality." So cut out sugared junk food and white sugar.

"Mucousless Diet Healing System," Arnold Ehrets.

"Born to Heal," Ruth Montgomery. Gives example of pouring much Apple Cider Vinegar on a woman "sprayed" with hot soup over a third of her body. Had 3rd degree burn on small place her girdle was padded. Attention airports and first aid stations.

"God Created Medicine out of the earth and caused them to grow for the service of Man."

D.C. Jarvis M.D., "Folk Medicine." Cider vinegar and honey have changed non-fertile man and beast to happy parents, made healthy hair, energy and rosy cheeks, etc."

"New Hope for Incurable Diseases," by E. Cheraskin M.D. and W.M. Ringsdorf Jr., M.D.

Dozens of cures with lemons. Western Front, P.O. Box 27854, Hollywood, CA 90027.

"Organic Consumer Report," Eden Ranch, Box 370, Topanga, CA 90290. Send stamped envelope for samples.

"Health Foods and Herbs," Katherine Hunter. Recipes and diets with herbs.

"Herb Growing for Health," Donald Law.

"Encyclopedia of Medicinal Herbs," Joseph Kadans, 256 pgs. Lists herbs by common and botanical names. Fifty pages, lists body's stress with herbs to relieve it. There are thirty healing uses of Comfrey, root and leaves: as for gout, kidney stones, asthma, arthritis, ulcers, sometimes as poultice.

"Proven Herbal Remedies," hardback by John H. Tobe, 304 pages, Provoker Press, St. Catherine, Ont., Canada. He lists 26 herbs that have cured cancer, such as clover blossom, dandelion root, parsley leaves, roots and seeds, grapes, the fruit and juice to purify the blood. Dr. Wm. Fox says, "Cancers are ulcers and proceed from poisons in the blood stream." A man with cancer of prostate returned after twice operated, sipped a quart of unsweetened pure grape juice mornings, eating lightly later, cured in two months.

There are teas to relax and induce sleep. But — don't relax your caution if you gather herbs yourself. By the highway and sprayed places they are polluted and could kill you. For safety get them from Health Food Stores or Herb Companies. Nutrition magazines advertise them. Heritage Store, PO Box 444B, Virginia Beach, VA 23458, sells herbs and Cayce's suggested formulas.

One of the most useful and exciting herbs was discovered and used for hundreds of years by our central U.S. Indians. We would have known it earlier if we'd been more friendly. They made tea from leaves of the Creosote bush to eradicate cancer, ulcers, arthritis and skin sores. Those who daily drank the tea made from it did not get sick. It has been researched and used for over 10 years and has no side effects. It can be used when taking other medicines. An eminent doctor of Arizona used it on his cancer patients for 8 years and says, "It's the best body builder I have. Growths seem to disappear, patients regain their strength and there is no cancer reaction in blood stream, gastric ulcers disappear, it normalizes the whole body."

If your health food store doesn't have it, tell them to order the pure air-dried and cold-pressed 15 grain tablet called "Chaparral" from Nature's Way Products, Box 2233, Provo, Utah 84601. My friend took 12 a day for the 6 days before a major operation and didn't need the operation. But even God cannot heal a person if he doesn't want it.

Books by Hanna Kroeger, MsD, registered nurse, nutritionist and researcher. "Old time Remedies for Modern Ailments," and "Vit-Mineral Locator," New Age Foods, 1122 Pearl

Boulder, Co. She operates a health resort where "miracles" happen. A paralyzed (from nickel deposits) person can take a tablespoon of poppyseed, in honey or tea, for about 8 weeks, twice a day and the paralysis is gone. Same dosage for epilepsy. She's seen that 6 tablets of Chaparral for 10 days by previous L.S.D. users cleared and renewed the body. Cleans the liver and blood stream. She's seen a nightly fresh-grated cabbage poultice around water-on-the-knee heal in four nights, or a fresh organic tomato poultice on an inoperable head tumor remove the tumor in 5 days. When that water is drawn out, the smell in the room is terrible and will get into mattress and clothing. Prepare for it.

Do get "Prevention" Magazine, Rodale Press, Inc., Emmaus, Pa. 18049. Their researched articles and letters to the Mailbag are priceless. A woman wrote that she cured her child's so called incurable cystic fibrosis (lung congestion) by adding to his diet 3 oz. of fresh carrot juice to 1 oz. of horseradish juice. A man ate a bowl of cherries and his gout disappeared, so he ate a few every day and it stayed away. Youths found their teeth straightening as they blew a wind instrument (how about a comb orchestra in kindergarten or 1st grade.) Types of arthritis should eat raw red Irish potatoes. Arthritis sufferers are low in Pantothenic acid. Aspirin kills pantothenic acid. Thus when pain reappears it's even worse. Artificial flavorings and colorings, carbonated drinks and synthetic sweetening are producing hyperactive nervous children. To lower blood pressure, sing loudly and breathe deeply. If this makes other pressure go up, then take silent deep breathing and eat garlic, or take garlic-parsley pearls. Warts and asthma have been cured by much Vitamin E, much (50,000 units) Vitamin A a day. If your animals have sores or infections or get lame give them the same as you give people — give them brewer's yeast powder or tablets and desiccated liver and they stay well and the fleas flee them.

Tests prove that synthetic Vitamins cannot feed cells. But your belief and sugar pills have — so save money. Doctors have found that lack of niacinimide causes premature senility.

Limit meals to 3 compatible foods. Never combine meat and milk, fruits and vegetables, or acid fruits and grain cereals. Between meals eat the other desired food. Acid jelly and bread is OUT.

Daily intake should be one-fourth protein starches, three-fourths vegetables and fruits.

Health Research (see page 193) has Food Charts.

Read books by authorities from your bookstore. I can't research for you. I'll send my findings with books — I'd appreciate yours. These findings may not be what you need — see your family doctor.

The address of a nutrition doctor closest to you can be obtained from: American Board of Nutrition, c/o Robert E. Hodges, M.D., Dept. of Medicine, University of California, Davis, CA 95616.

The Indian became wise in nature's ways by having hands, ears, and feet in contact with the earth. I was not surprised to learn that all three of these body surfaces are like charts connected to the centers of the whole human body and thus to the whole universe. The hands and feet have zones starting from the nails and ending with the torso at the wrists. The ear is an upsidedown picture of a baby body descending on earth head first, the lobe being the head. Now we know why a person trying to make up his mind massages the ear lobe, and why the staple on the stomach area of the ear makes your stomach think it's full. Do get this big thick book by the three M.D. Zone Therapists — Fitzgerald, White & Bowers. Order from A & M Book Center (M. Henderson), 22463 Detroit Rd, Rocky River, OH 46116.

"Painful menstruation, constipation and hemorrhoids yield to pressure of a probe or tongue depresser on the back wall of the pharynx. Apply the tongue depresser to the tongue ¾ of the way back, hold hand rigid and apply strong pressure for 2 minutes." Relax and move to another focus. Metal combing or hand-scratching the back of hands and the region of thumb and

1st and 2nd finger can do the job. If you are or desire to be pregnant, do not use the tongue pressure because abortion may follow. Use only finger pressures or comb for treatment.

A case of hand tremors, insomnia and exhaustion was successfully treated by putting wooden spring clothespins on the fingers daily for a week. Then 3 times more, 3 days apart.

For curing lumbago, press and squeeze the teeth of an aluminum "dog" comb on palms of hands and fingers. Continue for 10 to 20 minutes. (The back of the hand corresponds to the front of the body.)

For stomach sickness press the comb firmly over area near the thumb and forefinger and the web between. I have learned also that a piece of brown paper bag taped over the stomach and just above, prevents motion sickness — for dog or person.

Get a booklet on Dimethyl Sulfoxide (DMSO). It's the juice of trees when pulpwood is squeezed. It has been tested by medical doctors on 25,000 people since 1963, and has never hurt or caused side effects except for some temporary irritation. Six pages of this booklet are written by an M.D. who treated 2,000 test patients with marvelous results. It has been healing arthritis, varicose veins, mental retardation, mongolism, cancer, cataracts, burns, ulcers, Parkinson's disease, back problems including sprains, ruptured disc, shingles, kidney stones, multiple sclerosis, scar tissue, heart conditions — and the list is still growing. Only a few drops perform miracles. Many chemical companies have it — get the best grade. You may have to squeeze your own chopped-up tree because the F.D.A. is violently opposed to its use on people, but has approved it for veterinarians to use on animals. That is why this valuable booklet on DMSO is titled, *Or Would You Rather Be a Horse?*! Order it from I.C.R.F., 468 Ashford Ave., P.O. Box 97, Ardsley, NY 10502.

and saliva (2-hour old specimen would not do), they can see what's wrong in your body and prescribe the foods you should eat to become well. There is a small book about it, titled "Curse Causeless" (part of quote from Proverbs), from Independent C.S., P.O. Box 7031, Roanoke, VA 24019. A larger 108 page book on this subject is titled "Health Guide for Survival," by and from Salem Kirban Inc., 2117 Kent Rd., Huntingdon Valley, Penna., 19006, or from McCoys Health Center, Highway 120, Duluth, GA 30136.

QUOTES

"This book is a unique approach to the therapeutic use of signs and symbols of self as related to important people in our lives — Important in a way which can change one's image of self in relation to others. In my counseling work I have found it useful and successful for many."
Bella Karish, Fellowship of Universal Guidance, Los Angeles, Cal.

"Alice Steadman, a radiant person, proficient in the arts and in the art of living. She has shared her secrets of healthy living with those who read her book, "Who's the Matter With Me." Her keen insight into the causes of various troubles that bring on illness is remarkable. A blessing awaits you as you read this book."
— Genevieve Parkhurst, Author of "Healing the Whole Person".

"One cannot read 'Who's the Matter With Me?' without a consciousness that Alice Steadman is a very sensitive and honest person. She challenges old concepts, calls their bluff, and then shows that many must be challenged before their deep truths can be known.

She is not afraid of what she might find in the old or the new. Alice is "heady" wine — to be sipped at times and gulped

at others; either way she can help one to expand his own creativity."
R. Eugene Owens, Senior Minister, Myers Park Baptist Church, Charlotte, N.C.

"I was sowing such good deeds one day when I strained my back. I asked you what sort of God would do that to me. You let me realize that on that day the bad thought crop had come up to be harvested. You revealed the emotional hurt that triggered it." O. B. D.

"This is a valuable addition to my personal library." *Doctor and author of books on stress and disease.*

"This is 'Science of Mind' with a giggle." *Texas study group.*

"This book so vibrant with humor and ringing with the Truth so beautifully meets the human need."
Leslie A. Beaurline, Harrison, Arkansas

"A book for the Aquarian Age. Those who have suffered can find in it hope and healing. The young will understand it and be glad. Send me five dozen for the Ministry in the Marketplace."
George Colgin, minister of counseling, Winston-Salem, N.C.

"It was the privilege of our whole family to visit with the brilliant author of this book. We found her to be very sensible, very kind and very lovable in her creative insights. To live and think with her in the creative pages of this book can be most stimulating and rewarding."
Thomas A. Carruth, B.D., D.D.,

"Your wonderful book, 'Who's the Matter With Me?', has just been shared with me, and my love and grateful thanks go out to you for being the channel for such revealing Truth.

"This book has long been needed and you have the gift of expressing it in clear, beautiful words. So many dear souls need the realization that it is their words, thoughts, feelings, actions and reactions that build their world of happiness or unhappiness. You have explained it so beautifully. In blessing others with renewal of faith in God to bring forth abundance you are opening the way for His bountiful good to be poured out upon you. Christ lives and works in you and you are helping people realize that help is as close as His presence which is within them. I give thanks for your being the clear channel for this spirit of unity which links you with all people in a bond of fellowship for God and all mankind."

Mrs. Paul A. Jones, Unity Village, Lee's Summit, Mo.

"I like to tell my patients that of all the books I have put up for them to read, the one essential is yours because the philosophy is so beautifully expressed there and so particularly correct for dealing with chronic pain. Our Hospital Gift Shop keeps ordering them from you by the sixties." – *Dr. C. Norman Shealey, Director, Pain Rehabilitation Center, in La Crosse, WI.*

"I pay tribute to your blessed efforts to make this world enlightened and happier. Such a tremendous book. Fascinating, instructive and all priceless adjectives. Thank you for your inspiring book and God Bless you."

Elna M. Cuenco, Hulmeville, Pa.

"As I travel to meet with religious groups across the country it has been a joy to introduce your book. Many book tables at churches were interested in your offer in large quantities. It will be a fine and welcome addition and it will help so many people." *M.B., Florida*

"May I take this opportunity of telling you how inspiring and beneficial your book has been to me and to all who have received it. I am a student of yoga and I have found the basic tenets of the philosophy of yoga and all the philosophies incorporated very plainly, beautifully and simply in your book; the spirituality underlying all you say, particularly appeals to me."

Rose Rosenstone, Montreal, 20, Quebec

SUGGESTED READING

What's Right with the World, by Marcus Bach, Prentice-Hall.
The Stress of Life, by Hans Selye, M.D.
Your Mind Can Heal You, by F.W. Bailes
Your Mind Can Make You Sick or Well, Curt Wachtel, M.D.
Christ Liveth in Me, by Frank C. Laubach
Spiritual Therapy, by Dr. Richard Young
The Healing Light, by Agnes Sanford
Beyond the Darkness, by Stella Terrill Mann
Psychosomatic Medicine, by Weiss, Edward and English
Psychology, Religion and Healing, by Leslie Weatherhead
Living the Infinite Way, by Joel Goldsmith
Body and Mind, by Flanders Dunbar
Magic of Believing, by Claude Bristol
Three Magic Words, by U.S. Anderson
The Case of Unorthodox Medicine, by Brian Inglis
Emotional Stress and Your Health, by Brian Inglis
God Will Work With You But Not For You, by Lao Russell
   and *The Man Who Tapped the Secrets of the Universe,*
   by Glenn Clark (both from Uni. of Sci. & Phi., Swan-
   nanoa, Waynesville, Virginia)
All books by Glenn Clark, Macalester Press
Arthritis and Spiritual Laws, by Dr. Loring Swaim
Healing of Persons, by Paul Tournier
The Prophet, by Kahlil Gibran

The Story of Edgar Cayce, the Sleeping Prophet, by Jess
    Stearn, and *Search for God* (A.R.E., Virginia Beach, Va.)
As a Man Thinketh (DeVorss & Company)
Pathway to Contentment and *Everyday Counsel for Every-
    day Living* (combined), by Dr. Herbert Spaugh, D.D.,
    LL.D. (from Charlotte News, Charlotte, N.C.)
Our Unfailing Strength and other books on Prayer and
    Abundance. Louise Eggleston, World Literary Prayer
    Group, 900 Gates Ave., Norfolk 17, Va.
Jap Ji by Kirpal Singh
Think and Grow Rich, by Napoleon Hill.
The Health Secrets of a Naturopathic Doctor, M.O. Garten.
A Doctor's Thoughts on Healing, by Wm. S. Reid, M.D.
You Are Greater Than You Know. The Partnership Found-
    ation, Capon Springs, W.Va.
Psycho Cybernetics by Maxwell Maltz, M.D.

INDEX